Historical Collections Relating To The Potts Family In Great Britain And America V2

William John Potts

Historical Collections

RELATING TO

The Potts Family

IN

Great Britain and America

WITH A HISTORIC-GENEALOGY OF THE DESCENDANTS OF

David Potts

AN EARLY ANGLO-WELSH SETTLER OF PENNSYLVANIA

INCLUDING CONTRIBUTIONS BY THE LATE
WILLIAM JOHN POTTS

✿　✿　✿　✿　✿

COMPILED BY
THOMAS MAXWELL POTTS
Author of The Carter Family, Our Family Ancestors, etc.

CANONSBURG, PA.
PUBLISHED BY THE COMPILER
1901

CHAPTER VI.

Sixth Generation.

441 William C. Potts,[6] (John,[5] Thomas,[4] John,[3] John,[2] David,[1]), son of John and Elizabeth (Cooper) Potts, married Amanda Margerum. Residence, Philadelphia.

CHILDREN OF WILLIAM C. AND AMANDA (MARGERUM) POTTS.
1014 Benjamin Potts. There were also three daughters.

442 John R. Potts,[6] (John,[5] Thomas,[4] John,[3] John,[2] David,[1]), son of John and Elizabeth (Cooper) Potts, married Deborah Logan. Occupation, blacksmith. Residence, Moorestown.

CHILDREN OF JOHN R. AND DEBORAH (LOGAN) POTTS.
1015 John Potts.   1016 Clara Potts.

443 David B. Potts,[6] (John,[5] Thomas,[4] John,[3] John,[2] David,[1]), son of John and Elizabeth (Cooper) Potts, was a printer by trade, having served his apprenticeship upon the Germantown *Telegraph.* He edited the Chicopee (Mass.) *Herald* for sometime, and later established the Manyunk (Pa.) *Star.* He was twice married and left one daughter. He died about 1863.

447 William Cooper Potts,[6] (Thomas,[5] Thomas,[4] John,[3] John,[2] David,[1]), son of Thomas and Caroline (Cooper) Potts, was born 11 mo. 10, 1827. He married Phebe K. Walton, daughter of Jacob and Hannah Walton. He is a farmer and gardener and owns and occupies a portion of the land formerly owned by his great great grandfather, John

HORACE TURLEY POTTS.
PAGE 539.

Potts, in Upper Dublin Township, Montgomery County, and which has descended from father to son from generation to generation.

CHILDREN OF WILLIAM COOPER AND PHEBE K. (WALTON) POTTS.

1017 Thomas Elwood Potts. 1019 Caroline Potts.
1018 Dewberry Potts. 1020 Lydia W. Potts.

448 **Thomas Elwood Potts,**[6] (Thomas,[5] Thomas,[4] John,[8] John,[2] David,[1]), son of Thomas and Caroline (Cooper) Potts, was born 11 mo. 24, 1829. He married Rebecca Ruch. Residence, Upper Dublin Township, Montgomery County. Occupation, farmer.

CHILDREN OF THOMAS ELWOOD AND REBECCA (RUCH) POTTS.

1021 Forrest Potts, deceased. 1026 William Grant Potts.
1022 Frank Ruch Potts. 1027 John Potts, deceased.
1023 Elmer Ellsworth Potts. 1028 Charles Potts, deceased.
1024 Laura Amanda Potts. 1029 Ruch Potts.
1025 Emma Margaret Potts.

473 **Harriet Potts,**[6] (Thomas I.,[5] William L.,[4] Thomas,[8] John,[2] David,[1]), daughter of Thomas Isaac and Mary Frances (Johnson) Potts, married, first, William Potts Rockhill. During the Civil War he served with honor in Fifteenth Pennsylvania Cavalry, and was severely wounded in the Battle of Mumfreesboro. Residence, Pittstown, N. J. She married, second, Edward Yard Taylor.

CHILDREN OF WILLIAM POTTS AND HARRIET (POTTS) ROCKHILL.

1030 Edward Potts Rockhill.
1031 Anna Potts Rockhill.

474 **Horace Turley Potts,**[6] (Thomas I.,[5] William L.,[4] Thomas,[8] John,[2] David,[1]), son of Thomas Isaac and Mary Frances (Johnson) Potts, married Annie O'Harra, daughter of Harrison and Elizabeth (Miles) O'Harra.

CHILDREN OF HORACE TURLEY AND ANNIE (O'HARRA) POTTS.

1032 Harrison Isaac Potts. 1034 Helen Potts.
1033 Thomas Charles Potts. 1035 Horace Potts.

475   Kate B. Potts,[6] (Thomas I.,[5] William L.,[4] Thomas,[3] John,[2] David,[1]), daughter of Thomas Isaac and Mary Frances (Johnson) Potts, married Capt. Charles Hobbs, of the U. S. Navy.

CHILD OF CAPT. CHARLES AND KATE B. (POTTS) HOBBS.

1036   Horace Potts Hobbs.

477   Julia H. Potts,[6] (Charles C.,[5] William L.,[4] Thomas,[3] John,[2] David,[1]), daughter of Charles Clay and Mary J. (Ridgway) Potts, married Samuel H. Gray, son of Philip James and Sarah (Woolston) Gray, Sept. 25, 1862.   Mr. Gray is an able and accomplished attorney at law of high reputation, practicing in the Courts of New Jersey.

CHILDREN OF SAMUEL H. AND JULIA H. (POTTS) GRAY.

1037 Julia Ridgeway Gray.	1040 Ethel Gray.
1038 Charles Philip Gray.	1041 Alice Croasdale Gray.
1039 Mary J. Gray.	

481   Charles William Potts,[6] (William F.,[5] William L.,[4] Thomas,[3] John,[2] David,[1]), son of William Francis and Caroline (Tryon) Potts, was born July 25, 1848.   He married Adelaide Kelley, daughter of George W. and Mary Carey (Watson) Kelley, of Philadelphia.   She was born Dec. 11, 1849.   Mr. Potts succeeded his father as an Iron and Tin Merchant, on Market Street, Philadelphia.   He is Vice President of the Academy of Music ; a Director of the Girard National Bank ; Franklin Insurance Company ; City Trust, Safe Deposit and Surety Company ; and the Trades League of Philadelphia.   He is a Member of the Colonial Society of Pennsylvania ; the Historical Society of Pennsylvania ; Pennsylvania Sons of the Revolution ; the Netherland Society ; and Masonic Lodge, No. 51.   He is a Member of the following Clubs,—Union League, Art Club, Manufacturers Club, Sagwan Club, Country Club, and Bachelors Barge Club.

CHARLES WILLIAM POTTS.
PAGE 540.

482 **William John Potts,**[6] (Robert B.,[5] William L.,[4] Thomas,[3] John,[2] David,[1]), son of Robert Barnhill and Sarah Page (Grew) Potts, was born October 14, 1842, and died November 18, 1895. He received his education in the schools of Philadelphia and Camden, and studied chemistry in the University of Pennsylvania and in the Philadelphia Polytechnic College. He followed the profession of an Analytical Chemist for some years, but latterly devoted himself to literary and historical pursuits. He was a Member of American Philosophical Society; Historical Society of Pennsylvania; Historical Society of New England; New Jersey Historical Society; Numismatic and Antiquarian Society of Philadelphia; Pennsylvania Society of the Sons of the Revolution; and American Folk Lore Society; and a Corresponding Member of the Wisconsin Historical Society. Residence, Camden, New Jersey.

485 **Isabella Potts,**[6] (George H.,[5] Hugh H.,[4] Thomas,[3] John,[2] David,[1]), daughter of George H. and ——— (Cummings) Potts, married Dr. Joseph Lawrence Hicks, of Flushing, Long Island.

CHILDREN OF DR. JOSEPH L. AND ISABELLA (POTTS) HICKS.

1042 Isabella Hicks.   1043 Madge Hicks.   1044 Zelia Hicks.

486 **Hon. Frederick A. Potts,**[6] (George H.,[5] Hugh H.,[4] Thomas,[3] John,[2] David,[1]), son of George H, and ——— (Cummings) Potts, was born April 4, 1836, and died Nov. 9, 1888. He married Alice Brevoort. Mr. Potts was long identified with the coal and iron business in New York City, and latterly had control of a very large business as a Coal Merchant. In 1874 he was a Member of the Senate of New Jersey, from Hunterdon County. In 1878 he was the Republican candidate for Congress from the Fourth New Jersey District, known as the "Democratic Gibraltar." Such was his popularity that he was defeated by a majority of only 1500 in a district that had previously given a Democratic majority of 6500.   In 1880 he was the Republican Candidate for Governor of New Jersey and was only defeated by a majority of 651.   He was a person of fine physique and presence, strong character and genial disposition.

CHILDREN OF FREDERICK A. AND ALICE (BREVOORT) POTTS.

1045   A son.   1047   Rockhill Potts.
1046   William Potts.   1048   Meta Potts.

487   George C. Potts,[6] (George H.,[5] Hugh H.,[4] Thomas,[3] John,[2] David,[1]), son of George H. and ——— (Cummings) Potts, married, first, Mary Dallas, and second ——— Eustis.   He is a Broker of Philadelphia.

CHILDREN OF GEORGE C. AND MARY (DALLAS) POTTS.

1049   Hugh Potts.

488   Rockhill Potts,[6] (George H.,[5] Hugh H.,[4] Thomas.[3] John,[2] David,[1]), son of George H. and ——— (Cummings) Potts, married ——— Brevoort, a sister of his brother Frederick's wife.   He does business in New York.

CHILDREN OF ROCKHILL AND ——— (BREVOORT) POTTS.

1050   Robert Barnhill Potts.

505   Sarah Ann Hughs,[6] (Rachel,[5] James,[4] Samuel,[3] Daniel,[2] David,[1]), daughter of Eneas and Rachel (Potts) Hughs, was born 1804, and died May 1, 1893.   She married Robert Smith, son of John and grandson of Joseph Smith.   He was born 1804, and died February 7, 1885.   He was a blacksmith by trade, and for many years carried on smithing and farming near Gum Tree, Chester County.   After retiring from business the family removed to Coatesville.   They were Methodists in religious faith.

CHILDREN OF ROBERT AND SARAH ANN (HUGHS) SMITH.

1051   Eneas Franklin Smith, m. 1st, Esther Smith; 2d. Sarah E. Moon.
1052   Hannah Maria Smith, b. ——; d. June 13, 1875; m. R. Guthrie.
1053   John Smith, b. 1834; d. Oct. 30, 1843.
1054   Robert Smith, b. ——; d. Oct. 27, 1856.
1055   Rachel Emma Smith.   Residence, Coatesville, Pa.
1056   Samuel Wesley Smith, m. 1st, Lizzie Steen; 2d, Anna Boyer.

HON. FREDERICK A. POTTS.
PAGE 541.

506 Samuel Hughs,[6] (Rachel,[5] James,[4] Samuel,[3] Daniel,[2] David,[1]), son of Eneas and Rachel (Potts) Hughs, was born March —, 1807, and died July 4, 1881. He married Rachel Tarrance, daughter of James Tarrance. She was born about 1804, and died August 31, 1888. Occupation, farmer and tallow chandler. Residence, Highland Township, Chester County.

CHILDREN OF SAMUEL AND RACHEL (TARRANCE) HUGHS.

1057 Capt. James Hughs, b. 1832; d. Mar. 13, 1873; m. Mary Boyer.
1058 Rachel Ann Hughs, m. Theodore A. Baldwin.
1059 Sarah Jane Hughs, m. David Watterson.

507 Joseph Hughs,[6] (Rachel,[5] James[4] Samuel,[3] Daniel,[2] David,[1]), son of Eneas and Rachel (Potts) Hughs, was born March 11, 1810, and died June 18, 1880. He married, first, Sarah Craig, daughter of John Craig. He married, second, Emeline Swanscott. Occupation, carriage-maker. Residence, Georgetown, Lancaster County, and Gum Tree, Chester County, Pennsylvania, and Towsontown, near Baltimore, Maryland.

CHILDREN OF JOSEPH AND SARAH (CRAIG) HUGHS.

1060 John Eneas Hughs, d. y.
1061 Joseph Hughs, b. ——; d. Feb. —, 1895; m. Kate Swisher.
1062 Henry Hughs, b. ——; d. ——; m. Sarah Wright.
1063 Rachel Elizabeth Hughs. Residence, near Coatesville.
1064 Samuel Hughs. Married and resides in California.
1065 William Hughs.
1066 Sarah Ann Hughs, m. 1st, Frank Hamill; 2d. Dr. J. G. Gibson.

CHILDREN OF JOSEPH AND EMELINE (SWANSCOTT) HUGHS.

1067 John Hughs. Married and resides in Baltimore, Md.
1068 Mary Hughs. Married and resides in Baltimore, Md.

509 Eneas Hughs,[6] (Rachel,[5] James,[4] Samuel,[3] Daniel,[2] David,[1]), son of Eneas and Rachel (Potts) Hughs, was born 1816, and died Dec. 22, 1861. He married Eliza Pennock. Occupation, wheelwright. Residence, Highland Township, Chester County, Pennsylvania.

1069 Mary Louisa Hughs, m. Joel Harvey. Residence, Parkesburg.
1070 Eneas Franklin Hughs, m. Lettie Woods.
1071 S. Emma Hughs. m. Frank Tyler. Residence, Illinois.
1072 Charles W. Hughs.

510 Jesse Pearce Potts,[6] (James W.,[5] James,[4] Samuel,[3] Daniel,[2] David,[1]), son of James Wessell and Margaret (Stroud) Potts, was born March 14, 1813, in Chester County, Pennsylvania, and died August 1, 1859, in Dallas County, Iowa. He married Catharine Mann, daughter of Jacob and Ann Mann, Nov. 30, 1845, at Rochester, Cedar County, Iowa. Occupation, farmer.

CHILDREN OF JESSE AND CATHARINE (MANN) POTTS.

1073 Neve Potts, b. March 10, 1847; d. Nov. 25, 1863. He died in the Army in the Civil War, and his body taken home for burial.
1074 Louisa A. Potts, b. Dec. 12, 1848; m. George W. Wiandt.
1075 Brady Potts, b. May 21, 1850.
1076 Stephen Decatur Potts, b. Dec. 31, 1851.
1077 Franklin Pierce Potts, b. Nov. 13, 1853.
1078 Willey Potts, b. May 15, 1856; d. y.
1079 Joshua Potts, b. August 13, 1857.

512 Charlotte Potts,[6] (James W.,[5] James,[4] Samuel,[3] Daniel,[2] David,[1]), daughter of James Wessell aud Margaret (Stroud) Potts, was born 1816, in Chester County, Pennsylvania, and died June 18, 1850, in Iowa. She married John Scott. Residence, Masons Grove, Iowa.

CHILDREN OF JOHN AND CHARLOTTE (POTTS) SCOTT.

1080 Boon Scott, b. 1841.   1082 Phebe Scott, b. 1846.
1081 Mary Louisa Scott, b, 1843. 1083 Louisa Scott, b.

513 Sarah Louisa Potts,[6] (James W.,[5] James,[4] Samuel,[3] Daniel,[2] David,[1]), daughter of James Wessell and Margaret (Stroud) Potts, was born Dec. 12, 1817, in Chester County, Pennsylvania, and died Aug. 20, 1844, in LaPorte County, Indiana. She married Jesse Collom, son of Benjamin and Martha Collom, Jan. 20, 1845, in Erie County, Pa.

After the death of his wife, Sarah Louisa, he married Phebe
Potts, her younger sister. He was born Jan. 20, 1813, and
died Sept. 5, 1859. Occupation, farmer. Residence, La-
Porte County, Indiana.

CHILDREN OF JESSE AND SARAH LOUISA (POTTS) COLLOM.

1084 Martha J. Collom, b. April 10, 1838; d. Nov. 20, 1864.
1085 William Collom, b. Sept. 27, 1840; m.

514 Margaret Potts,[6] (James W.,[5] James,[4] Samuel,[3]
Daniel,[2] David,[1]), daughter of James Wessell and Margaret
(Stroud) Potts, was born 1819, in Chester County, Penn-
sylvania, and died June 14, 1849, in Cedar County, Iowa.
She married William Baker, son of Martin and Catharine
Baker, May 18, 1844. He was a merchant and farmer.

CHILDREN OF WILLIAM AND MARGARET (POTTS) BAKER.

1086 James Perry Baker, b. 1845.
1087 Welcome Martin Baker.

517 Phebe Potts,[6] (James W.,[5] James,[4] Samuel,[3] Daniel,[2] David,[1]) daughter of James Wessell and Margaret
(Stroud) Potts, was born January 18, 1824, and died Jan. 4,
1882. She married, first, Jesse Collom, Nov. 20, 1846, in
Cedar County, Iowa. (See No. 513). She married, second, David Ostrander. Residence, Mill Creek, LaPorte
County, Indiana.

CHILDREN OF JESSE AND PHEBE (POTTS) COLLOM.

1088 Catharine A. Collom, b. Feb. 20, 1848; d. Aug. 28, 1849.
1089 James W. Collom, b. January 20, 1850.
1090 George Washington Collom, b. March 6, 1852.

CHILDREN OF DAVID AND PHEBE (POTTS) OSTRANDER.

1091 Belle Ostrander, b. 1866.
1092 Gough Ostrander, b. 1869.

518 Sarah Louisa McIntire,[6] (Ann,[5] James,[4] Samuel,[3]
Daniel,[2] David,[1]), daughter of Thomas and Ann (Potts)
McIntire, was born August 9, 1817. She married John

69

Lash, son of Philip Lash, April 6, 1844. He was a carpenter and builder. Residence for many years, Bellville, and later, Mansfield, Ohio.

CHILDREN OF JOHN AND SARAH LOUISA (McINTIRE) LASH.

1093   Mary Virginia Lash, b. Jan, 15, 1845; d. May 4, 1849.
1094   Benjamin M. Lash, b. May 10, 1847; m. Emma Herron.
1095   Ann Elizabeth Lash, b. Dec. 7, 1850; deceased.
1096   Alfred Lash, b. Dec. 18, 1852; m. Mary Allen.
1097   Albert Scott Lash, b. Dec. 18, 1852; d. Aug. 28, 1856.

519   John Wessell McIntire,[6] (Ann,[5] James,[4] Samuel,[3] Daniel,[2] David,[1]), son of Thomas and Ann (Potts) McIntire, was born March 12, 1819, and died March 22, 1889. He married Ruth Weagley, daughter of Samuel and Ellen Weagley, September 20, 1853. Occupation, farmer. Residence, The Ridge, near Lexington, Richland County, Ohio.

CHILDREN OF JOHN W. AND RUTH (WEAGLEY) McINTIRE.

1098   Amanda McIntire, b. Sept. 4, 1854; m. William Wintersteen.
1099   Mary Elizabeth McIntire, b. Sept. 28, 1855; d. Jan. 3, 1882.
1100   Samuel Weagley McIntire, b. June 25, 1857; m. Ellen Geary.
1101   Ada Louisa McIntire, b. Nov. 7, 1858; d. March 18, 1859.
1102   Della McIntire, b. Dec. 8, 1859; m. Walter Graham.
1103   Margaret McIntire, b. Dec. 19, 1861; d. July 20, 1862.
1104   Margaret Williams McIntire, b. Sept. 2, 1863.
1105   Ellen McIntire, b. Oct. 4, 1865; deceased.
1106   John McIntire, b. May 2, 1867.
1107   May McIntire, b. August 10, 1869.

522   Margaret E. McIntire,[6] (Ann,[5] James,[4] Samuel,[3] Daniel,[2] David,[1]), daughter of Thomas and Ann (Potts) McIntire, was born August 4, 1825. She married Thomas Dunshee. He was born ——, and died June 1, 1889. Occupation, farmer. Residence, Lexington, Ohio.

CHILD OF THOMAS AND MARGARET E. (McINTIRE) DUNSHEE.

1108   Thomas Eugene Dunshee, b. Aug. 20, 1854; m. Adella Cleland.

524   Sarah Ann Potts,[6] (Samuel,[5] James,[4] Samuel,[3] Daniel,[2] David,[1]), daughter of Samuel and Margaret (Sheaf-

JAMES CARTER POTTS.
PAGE 549.

er) Potts, was born Sept. 17, 1817, and died Dec. 12, 1893.
She married Jacob Leiby, son of Jacob and —— (Lambert)
Leiby, 1841.   He was born Sept 10, 1806, and died May 20,
1885.   Occupation, brewer and stock dealer.   Residence,
Carlisle and Middletown, Pennsylvania.

CHILDREN OF JACOB AND SARAH ANN (POTTS) LEIBY.

1109 Samuel Leiby, b. Nov. 19, 1841; d. May 10, 1842.
1110 Anna Leiby, b. Oct. 19, 1843; m. Samuel Mumma.
1111 Ella Leiby, b. April 22, 1845; m. John W. Few.
1112 Araballa Leiby, b. Sept. 23, 1846; m. John W. Rife.
1113 Elizabeth Leiby, b. May 12, 1850; d. June 6, 1860.
1114 Catharine Leiby, b. May 12, 1850; m. Samuel Singer.
1115 Thomas Leiby, b. March 9, 1853; d. May 16, 1855.
1116 William Leiby. b. Jan. 9, 1856; m. Louisa D. Shurer.

525 James Potts,[6] (Samuel,[5] James,[4] Samuel,[3] Daniel,[2]
David,[1]), son of Samuel and Margaret (Sheafer) Potts, was
born 1820, and died August 28, 1886.   He married Mary
Mulford, daughter of Jonathan and Ann Mulford.   She was
born ——, and died September —, 1887.   He was a coach-
maker and machinest by trade, but engaged in merchandiz-
ing and accumulated a considerable fortune.   He was a
public spirited man and an active church worker in the
Methodist Episcopal denomination.   Residence, Lancaster,
Pennsylvania.

CHILDREN OF JAMES AND MARY (MULFORD) POTTS.

1117 Andrew R. Potts, d. y.   1119 James Potts, d. y.
1118 James Bernard Potts, d. y.   1120 Sarah Jane Potts.

526 Thomas Maxwell Potts,[6] (Thomas J.,[5] James,[4]
Samuel,[3] Daniel,[2] David,[1]) son of Thomas Jefferson and
Margaret (Carter) Potts, was born February 17, 1836, in
(now) Highland Township, Chester County, Pennsylvania.
He married Mary Miller,* daughter of Reuben and Sarah

---

* THE MILLER FAMILY. Gayen Miller settled at Kennett, Chester County, Pa.,
about or shortly after the year 1700. His wife was Margaret Henderson. They
had twelve children. Joseph, the ninth child, married Jane Kirk, daughter of Jacob. Their son Samuel married Martha Hobson, daughter of Francis. Their son
Samuel married Margaret Mitchel, daughter of Richard or John. Their son Reuben married Sarah Baker, daughter of John. [See OUR FAMILY ANCESTORS].

(Baker) Miller, March 22, 1860. She was born April 6,
1838. He received his education in the schools of Chester
County and at the Normal School at Millersville, Lancaster
County. He taught school in the Academy at Downingtown, and Greenwood Seminary at Millville, in Pennsylva-
vania ; and as Principal and Superintendant of the Public
Schools of Bellville, Ohio. He was engaged in the retail
hardware trade for sometime at Bellville, Ohio, and at Canonsburg, Pennsylvania.

Having learned the printing trade, he opened an office at
Canonsburg in 1870, and in 1872 established the *Canonsburg
Herald*, a weekly newspaper, which he conducted until
1888. He published *A Short Biographical Sketch of Major
James Potts*, in 1877 ; *Bi-Centenary Memorial of Jeremiah
Carter*, in 1883 ; and *Our Family Ancestors*, in 1895. He
edited Volumes I, II, III, and IV, of the *Register* of the
National Delaine Merino Sheep Breeders Association ; and
Volumes I and II of the *Record* of the Improved Black-Top
Merino Sheep Breeders Association ; has contributed to oth-
er publications ; and is the publisher of the present work.

He has held several local offices, School Director, Member of Town Council, Borough Treasurer, Burgess, Mayor,
and now holds his fourth commission as Justice of the Peace.
He is a Ruling Elder and Superintendent of the Sabbath
School of the First Presbyterian Church of Canonsburg.
He is a Past Grand and Past Chief Patriarch of the Odd
Fellows, and a Past Regent of the Royal Arcanum. He
is a Life Member of the Canonsburg Library Association
and its President since 1880, and a Corresponding Member
of the New England Historic Genealogical Society. Residence, Canonsburg. Pennsylvania.

CHILDREN OF THOMAS MAXWELL AND MARY (MILLER) POTTS.

1121   Reuben Claude Potts, b. Jan. 25, 1861; m. Sarah Claribel Fife.
1122   Rev. Thomas Pliny Potts, A. M., b. Oct. 23, 1862.
1123   William Baker Potts, b. March 6, 1865.
1124   Mitchel Miller Potts, b. Jan. 5, 1867; m. Sarah Grace Beatty.
1125   Louis Maxwell Potts, A. B., Ph. D., b. Oct. 30, 1876.

WILLIAM POTTS.
PAGE 549.

527 James Carter Potts,[6] (Thomas J.,[5] James,[4] Samuel,[3] Daniel,[2] David,[1]), son of Thomas Jefferson and Margaret (Carter) Potts, was born June 24, 1837, in (now) Highland Township, Chester County, Pennsylvania. He married Grizelle McIntire, (523), daughter of Thomas and Ann (Potts) McIntire, September 13, 1860, and settled at Bellville, Richland County, Ohio. He is a druggist and surveyor. He conducted a drug-store at Bellville, for many years in connection with a printing office. In 1872 he established the *Bellville Dollar Weekly*, a newspaper, which he continued to publish until 1881, when he disposed of it on account of ill health. He has filled the office of County Surveyor for several successive terms. He was instrumental in establishing a local telephone system in his town and community. He held the office Postmaster of Bellville for one term. He is a Ruling Elder and was long Superintendent of the Sabbath School of the Bellville Presbyterian Church. Residence, Bellville, Ohio.

CHILDREN OF JAMES CARTER AND GRIZELLE (McINTIRE) POTTS.

1126 Anna Eudora Margaret Potts, b. Sep. 17, 1861; m. Rob. Castner.
1127 Mary Louisa Potts, b. Jan. 6, 1864; d. Sept. 18, 1865.
1128 Harry Lee Potts, b. April 5, 1866; m. —— Hamilton.
1129 Linnie May Potts, b. April 5, 1866; m. Dr Mahlon Blair.

529 William Potts,[6] (Thomas J.,[5] James,[4] Samuel,[3] Daniel,[2] David,[1]), son of Thomas Jefferson and Margaret (Carter) Potts, was born January 15, 1843, in (now) Highland Township, Chester County, Pa. He married Anna L. Wilson, daughter of Reuben and Sarah (Eves) Wilson, of Millville, Columbia County, Dec. 16, 1875, by Friends ceremony, at the home of the bride's parents. He succeeded to the homestead in Highland Township, where he conducts the farm and manages a steam saw-mill which he has erected on the premises. He is a Ruling Elder in Faggs Manor Presbyterian Church, and Superintendent of the Fairview Sabbath School. He is an active member of Highland Grange of the P of H. Postoffice, Parkesburg, Penna.

1130 Mary Etta Potts, b. Oct. 28, 1876.
1131 Thomas Wilson Potts, b. Oct. 27, 1880.

530 Joseph Tarrance Potts,[6] (Thomas J.,[5] James,[4] Samuel,[3] Daniel,[2] David,[1]), son of Thomas Jefferson and Margaret (Carter) Potts, was born August 24, 1845, in (now) Highland Township, Chester County. He married Mary Elizabeth Hamill, daughter of Elisha and Mary (Kerr) Hamill, Jan. 8, 1873. He is a farmer and resides about one and a half miles from the homestead. He has had some success in the cultivation of small fruits. He is also engaged in the manufacture of brooms. He is a practical surveyor. He is a Presbyterian in church connection, and a member of Highland Grange of the Patrons of Husbandry. Postoffice, Cochranville, Penna.

CHILDREN OF JOSEPH T. AND M. ELIZABETH (HAMILL) POTTS.
1132 Nellie Louisa Potts, b. Feb. 5, 1874.
1133 Joseph Edgar Potts, b. March 7, 1876; d. July 11, 1876.
1134 Charles Edwin Potts, b. June 11, 1877.
1135 Mary Bertha Potts, b. March 6, 1880.
1136 Anna Marguerite Potts, b. Jan. 27, 1897.

532 Alfred Hamilton Potts,[6] (Thomas J.,[5] James,[4] Samuel,[3] Daniel,[2] David,[1]), son of Thomas Jefferson and Margaret (Carter) Potts, was born June 17, 1853, in (now) Highland Township, Chester County. He married Alice Young, daughter of A. Philip and Rachel (Wilson) Young, of Millville, Columbia County, Pa., August 21, 1884. He learned the trade of a tinner and roofer. Later he became a clerk in his brother's drug store, at Bellville, O., and assisted in editing the *Bellville Weekly*. In 1874 he purchased a printing office at Parkesburg, Chester County, Pa. He has since conducted a large printing and publishing business at that place. He has published *American Stock Journal*, the *Farmers Magazine and Rural Guide*, the *Poultry Keeper*, and the *Chester County Times*. A large

JOSEPH TARRANCE POTTS.
PAGE 550.

number of other periodicals, weekly and monthly, are and have been printed at this office as well as an extensive jobbing business. He has a small farm, a part of the homestead, about four miles south of Parkesburg, where he resides. He is an active worker in the Presbyterian church, and a Sabbath School Superintendent. He is a member of Highland Grange of the Patrons of Husbandry.'

CHILDREN OF ALFRED HAMILTON AND ALICE (YOUNG) POTTS.

1137 Alfred Hamilton Potts, Jr., b. Jan. 18, 1889; d. Jan. 19, 1889.
1138 Margaret Reinee Potts, b. April 6, 1890.
1139 Philip Clive Potts, b. Feb. 25, 1892.
1140 Rachel Inez Potts, b. Sept. 19, 1895.
1141 Stella Henrietta Potts, b. August 29, 1897.
1142 Zella Marietta Potts, b. August 29, 1897.

538   Sarah Benham Potts,[6] (Jesse C.,[5] Jesse,[4] Samuel,[5] Daniel,[2] David,[1]), daughter of Jesse Charles and Eunice U. (Walker) Potts, was born August 11, 1837, in Albany, N.Y. She is a graduate of the Albany Female Academy. She is active in religious and charitable work, and is a Patroness and Manager of the Albany Hospital Training School for Nurses, and a Member of St. Peter's Protestant Episcopal Church of Albany.

539   Jesse Walker Potts,[6] (Jesse Charles,[5] Jesse,[4] Samuel,[3] Daniel,[2] David,[1]), son of Jesse Charles and Eunice U. (Walker) Potts, was born November 4, 1843, in Albany, N. Y. After attending Wrightson's Select School, and the Albany Academy, he entered Harvard University and graduated in the Class of 1865, and was a Member of the Phi Beta Kappa Society. He is an active public-spirited man, and is a Governor of the Albany Hospital ; a Trustee of the Albany Medical College ; a Trustee and Secretary of the Home for Aged Men ; a Director of the Albany Institute and Historical and Art Society ; a Trustee and Vice President of the Guild House and Institute of Charity, and a Vestryman of St. Peter's Church.   He is a Member of the

Fort Orange Club; of the Albany Camera Club; of the Harvard Club of New York City; of the Harvard Club of Eastern and Central New York; and a Life Member of the American Numismatic and Archæological Society.   Both he and his sister are unmarried and reside at No. 342 State Street, Albany.   In 1895, he and his sister erected and presented to St. Peter's Church a fine Rectory, as a Memorial to their father and mother.

54b **William Potts,[6]** (Charles D.,[5] William E.,[4] Daniel,[3] Daniel,[2] David,[1]), son of Charles D. and Mary Ann (Opdyke) Potts, was born August 18, 1829.   He married Malinda Spindler, daughter of John Spindler, Oct. 27, 1853. He is a carpenter and joiner.   Residence, Kingston Center, Delaware County, Ohio.

CHILDREN OF WILLIAM AND MALINDA (SPINDLER) POTTS.

1143   John Wesley Potts, b. Dec. 27, 1854.
1144   James B. Potts, b. March 29, 1857.
1145   Mary Jane Potts, b. July 25, 1859.
1146   Charles Potts, b. Feb. 8, 1862.
1147   Lenna Potts, b. Feb. 6, 1865.
1148   George Allen Potts, b. Oct. 18, 1867.
1149   William Frederick Potts, b. Sept. 22, 1871.

542   **Benjamin J. Potts,[6]** (Charles D.,[5] William E.,[4] Daniel,[3] Daniel,[2] David,[1]), son of Charles D. and Mary Ann (Opdyke) Potts, was born October 13, 1833, in Hunterdon County, New Jersey.   He married Mary Meredith, daughter of James and Rachel Meredith, May 8, 1860.   Occupation, carpenter and builder.   He filled the office of Infirmary Director of Morrow County for two terms.   Residence, Andrews, Morrow County, Ohio.

CHILDREN OF BENJAMIN J. AND MARY (MEREDITH) POTTS.

1150   Laura Augusta Potts, b. Dec. 15, 1861.
1151   Clifton Meredith Potts, b. Dec. 25, 1868.

543   **Joseph Potts,[6]** (Charles D.,[5] William E.,[4] Daniel.[3]

ALFRED H. POTTS.   ALICE Y. POTTS.
PHILIP CLIVE POTTS.   MARGARET REINEE POTTS
RACHEL INEZ POTTS.
ZELLA MARIETTA POTTS.   STELLA HENRIETTA POTTS.
PAGE 550.

Daniel,² David,¹), son of Charles D. and Mary Ann (Opdyke) Potts, was born Feb. 10, 1836. He married Isabella Ralston, daughter of John Ralston, Oct. 16, 1858. Residence, Mt. Gilead, Morrow County, Ohio.

CHILDREN OF JOSEPH AND ISABELLA (RALSTON) POTTS.

1152 Charles Bartley Potts, b. April 19, 1860.
1153 Minnie Potts, b. Aug. 19, 1871; d. Feb. 9, 1878.
1154 Carrie Potts, b. July 7, 1894.

545 Daniel W. Potts,⁶ (Charles D.,⁵ William E.,⁴ Daniel,³ Daniel,² David,¹), son of Charles D. and Mary Ann (Opdyke) Potts, was born Nov. 24, 1840. He married Arrilla Lewis, daughter of Eliphalet and Evaline (Fish) Lewis, Oct. 3, 1869. She was born Sept. 24, 1851. He served for a term of three years during the Civil War in the 81st Regiment, Ohio Volunteer Infantry. Residence, Sparta, Morrow County, Ohio.

CHILDREN OF DANIEL W. AND ARRILLA (LEWIS) POTTS.

1155 Nellie Potts, b. May 23, 1871.
1156 Lewis Potts, b. May 5, 1874.
1157 Sarah Potts, b. Feb. 26, 1877.
1158 Jennie Potts, b. Jan. 18, 1885.

548 Mary D. Potts,⁶ (Charles D.,⁵ William E.,⁴ Daniel,³ Daniel,² David,¹), daughter of Charles D. and Mary A. (Opdyke) Potts, was born March 15, 1849, and died Oct. 10, 1885. She married Morgan Howard, son of John and Mary (James) Howard, Nov. 14, 1868. Residence, Marengo Morrow County, Ohio.

CHILDREN OF MORGAN AND MARY D. (POTTS) HOWARD.

1159 Ora Howard, b. August 4, 1869.
1160 Milo C. Howard, b. Jan. 1, 1875.
1161 Ellis A. Howard, b. Dec. 29, 1880.

549 Susan Potts,⁶ (Joseph,⁵ William E.,⁴ Daniel,³ Daniel,² David,¹), daughter of Joseph and Catharine (Manning)

70

Potts, was born Dec. 28, 1838.   She married George S. Cole, Oct. 12, 1859.   Residence, Hunterdon County, N. J.

CHILDREN OF GEORGE S. AND SUSAN (POTTS) COLE.

1162 Joseph Potts Cole, b. Oct. 20, 1860; d. Sept. 21, 1862.
1163 Simon P. Cole, b. Sept. 2, 1862.
1164 Eugene Cole, b. July 26, 1864.
1165 Stephen E. Cole, b. March 16, 1866.
1166 Bertha Cole, b. October 27, 1868.
1167 Benjamin Cole, b. January 19, 1871.
1168 Georgie Cole, b. May 17, 1873.
1169 Kate R. Cole, b. November 23, 1875.

550 Christiana Potts,[6] (Joseph,[5] William E.,[1] Daniel,[3] Daniel,[2] David,[1]), daughter of Joseph and Catharine (Manning) Potts, was born May 17, 1840.   She married Philip Bosenbury, October 15, 1867.   Residence, Hunterdon Co., New Jersey.

CHILDREN OF PHILIP AND CHRISTIANA (POTTS) BOSENBURY.

1170 Philip Bosenbury, b. January 11, 1869.
1171 Mary Bosenbury, b. January 14, 1872.

551 Mary Potts,[6] (Joseph,[5] William E.,[4] Daniel,[3] Daniel,[2] David,[1]), daughter of Joseph and Catharine (Manning) Potts, was born Dec. 27, 1843.   She married Horace Prall Quick, Aug. 18, 1864.   Residence, Hunterdon County, N.J.

CHILD OF HORACE PRALL AND MARY (POTTS) QUICK.

1172 Lada Quick, b. November 22, 1868.

552 Jane Potts,[6] (Joseph,[5] William E.,[4] Daniel,[3] Daniel,[2] David,[1]), daughter of Joseph and Catharine (Manning) Potts, was born Oct. 29, 1846.   She married Henry P. VanFleet, May 27, 1871.   Residence, Hunterdon County, N.J.

CHILD OF HENRY P. AND JANE (POTTS) VANFLEET.

1173 Luella VanFleet, b. July 26, 1873.

553 Martha Potts,[6] (Joseph,[5] William E.,[4] Daniel,[3] Daniel,[2] David,[1]), daughter of Joseph and Catharine (Manning) Potts, was born Dec. 15, 1848. She married John Hoffman, Dec. 27, 1870. Residence, Hunterdon Co., N. J.

CHILD OF JOHN AND MARTHA (POTTS) HOFFMAN.

1174 Mary Hoffman, b. March 19, 1874.

558 Catharine Potts,[6] (Daniel E.,[5] William E.,[4] Daniel,[3] Daniel,[2] David,[1]), daughter of Daniel E. and Alletta (Rockafellow) Potts, was born Feb. 6, 1844. She married John Park, Dec. 9, 1868. Residence, Hunterdon Co., N. J.

CHILDREN OF JOHN AND CATHARINE (POTTS) PARK.

1175 George E. Park, b. January 29, 1870.
1176 Fannie B. Park, b. October 22, 1873.

560 John Potts,[6] (Daniel E.,[5] William E.,[4] Daniel,[3] Daniel,[2] David,[1]), son of Daniel E. and Alletta (Rockafellow) Potts, was born June 26, 1847. He married Jane Cook, Feb. 19, 1875. Residence, Hunterdon County, N. J.

CHILDREN OF JOHN AND JANE (COOK) POTTS.

1177 George W. Potts, b. November 22, 1875.

565 Isaac Walker,[6] (Mary,[5] Elizabeth,[4] Peter,[3] Elizabeth,[2] David,[1]), son of Asahel and Mary (Vale) Walker, was born 7 mo. 13, 1808. He married Rebecca ——, 3 mo. 4, 1834.

CHILDREN OF ISAAC AND REBECCA (——) WALKER.

1178 Asahel Walker, b. 1 mo. 8, 1836.
1179 Peter D. Walker, b. 7 mo. 13, 1837.
1180 Julia Ann Walker, b. 12 mo. 22, 1838.
1181 Alfred Walker, b. 3 mo. 5, 1841.
1182 Lewis Walker, b. 11 mo. 18, 1844.
1183 Enos Walker, b. 3 mo. 17, 1845.
1184 Morris Walker, b. 2 mo. 20, 1848.
1185 Rebecca Jane Walker, b. 12 mo. 19, 1851.
1186 Isaac S. Walker, b. 6 mo. 26, 1853.

566 Elizabeth Walker,[6] (Mary,[5] Elizabeth,[4] Peter,[3] Elizabeth,[2] David,[1]), daughter of Asahel and Mary (Vale)

Walker, was born 9 mo. 1, 1810. She married George W. Cook, 8 mo. 30, 1832.

CHILDREN OF GEORGE W. AND ELIZABETH (WALKER) COOK.

1187 Asahel Walker Cook, m. Hannah C. Garretson.

1188 Maria Jane Cook.	1192 Samuel Cook.
1189 Sarah Ann Cook.	1193 Theodore Cook.
1190 Mary Cook.	1194 Jessie Cook.
1191 Georgiana Cook.	1195 Ruth Emma Cook.

567 **Priscilla Walker,**[6] (Mary,[5] Elizabeth,[4] Peter,[3] Elizabeth,[2] David,[1]), daughter of Asahel and Mary (Vale) Walker, was born 7 mo. 14, 1814. She married William Hoopes, 12 mo. 15, 1831.

CHILDREN OF WILLIAM AND PRISCILLA (WALKER) HOOPES.

1196 Mary Hoopes.	1199 John Hoopes.
1197 Asahel Hoopes.	1200 Elizabeth Ann Hoopes.
1198 Jane Hoopes.	

568 **Louisa Walker,**[6] (Mary,[5] Elizabeth,[4] Peter,[3] Elizabeth,[2] David,[1]), daughter of Asahel and Mary (Vale) Walker, was born 7 mo. 14, 1814. She married Isaac Garretson, 8 mo. 14, 1834.

CHILDREN OF ISAAC AND LOUISA (WALKER) GARRETSON.

1201 Amanda Garretson.	1204 Mary Garretson.
1202 Martha Garretson.	1205 Lydia Garretson.
1203 Theodore Garretson.	

570 **Morris E. Walker,**[6] (Mary,[5] Elizabeth,[4] Peter,[3] Elizabeth,[2] David,[1]), son of Asahel and Mary (Vale) Walker, was born 2 mo. 16, 1820. He married Jane ————.

CHILDREN OF MORRIS E. AND JANE (————) WALKER.

1206 Charles P. Walker.	1209 Emma Walker.
1207 Jane Walker.	1210 Asahel W. Walker.
1208 Lydia Walker.	1211 Warren B. Walker.

571 **Joshua Vale Walker,**[6] (Mary,[5] Elizabeth,[4] Peter,[3] Elizabeth,[2] David,[1]), son of Asahel and Mary (Vale) Walker, was born 11 mo. 3, 1822. He married Elizabeth ————.

CHILDREN OF JOSHUA VALE AND ELIZABETH (——↓——) WALKER.

1212   George Walker.   1213   Mary Walker.

572   **Sarah Walker,**[6] (Mary,[5] Elizabeth,[4] Peter,[3] Elizabeth,[2] David,[1]), daughter of Asahel and Mary (Vale) Walker, was born 4 mo. 1, 1827.   She married John G. Brown.

CHILDREN OF JOHN G. AND SARAH (WALKER) BROWN.

1214   Priscilla W. Brown.   1218   Joel Brown.
1215   Susanna Brown.   1219   Millin Thomas Brown.
1216   Mary Ellen Brown.   1220   Asahel W. Brown.
1217   Joseph B. Brown.   1221   David Walter Brown.

593   **Isaac Vale,**[6] (Martha,[5] John,[4] Peter,[3] Elizabeth,[2] David,[1]), son of Robert and Martha (Cleaver) Vale, was born 2 mo, 1, 1813.   He married Mary Ann Walker (569) daughter of Asahel and Mary (Vale) Walker, 10 mo. 26, 1837, at Warrington, York County, Pennsylvania.   Residence, Webber, Kansas.

CHILDREN OF ISAAC AND MARY ANN (WALKER) VALE.

1222   John C. Vale, b. 8 mo. 22, 1838; d. 12 mo. 9, 1862.
1223   Eli Vale, b. 11 mo. 19, 1840; m. Rebecca Starr, 1871.
1224   Eliza Ann Vale, b. 5 mo. 14, 1842; m. H. H. Sidwell, 1866.
1225   Asahel Walker Vale, b. 2 mo. 20, 1844; m. Sarah E. Mills.
1226   Robert Amos Vale, b. 2 mo. 24, 1846; m. 1st, Hannah Eisemmann, 1876; 2d, Mary Tomlinson, 1890.
1227   Nathan·C. Vale, b. 1 mo. 20, 1848; m. Martha E. Mills, 1877.
1228   Isaac Edwin Vale, b. 5 mo. 19, 1852; m. Hannah E. Shore.
1229   Mary E. Vale, b. 2 mo. 25, 1858; m. William W. Gunn, 1879.

599   **Amos G. Cleaver,**[6] (John,[5] John,[4] Peter,[3] Elizabeth,[2] David,[1]), son of John and Ann (Vale) Cleaver, was born 1815, and died March 12, 1900.   He married Amelia Morris, daughter of Samuel and Jennie (Sturgeon) Morris, Feb. 4, 1837.   She was born 1818.   Occupation, first, tanner, and lastly farmer.   Residence, West Pike Run Township, Washington County, Penna.

CHILDREN OF AMOS G. AND AMELIA (MORRIS) CLEAVER.

1230   Lewis M. Cleaver, b. Nov. 14, 1837; m. —— ——.   No issue.

1231 Annie C. Cleaver, b. May 2, 1841; m. Ahira Jones.
1232 Hiram T. Cleaver, b. Nov. 20, 1843.
1233 William H. Cleaver, b. Feb. 3, 1846.
1234 Elizabeth Cleaver, b. June 17, 1848.
1235 Samuel M. Cleaver, b. April 18, 1851.
1236 John W. Cleaver, b. Sept. 27, 1863.

600 Eli V. Cleaver,[6] (John,[5] John,[4] Peter,[3] Elizabeth,[2] David,[1]), son of John and Ann (Vale) Cleaver, was born 1816, and died 1881. He married Rebecca Bracken, daughter of Solomen Bracken, 1839. He was a tanner by trade, but engaged in farming and mercantile pursuits. He was a Member of the Ohio Legislature for two terms.

CHILDREN OF ELI V. AND REBECCA (BRACKEN) CLEAVER.

1237 Anna Cleaver, b. 1840.   1240 Oliver R. Cleaver, b 1861.
1238 Ella Cleaver, b. 1852.   1241 Amelia Cleaver, b. 1865.
1239 Clara Cleaver, b. 1856.

601 Isaac N. Cleaver,[6] (John,[5] John,[4] Peter,[3] Elizabeth,[2] David,[1]), son of John and Ann (Vale) Cleaver, was born 1820, and died 1864. He married Isabel M. Dutton, daughter of David and Mary (Rogers) Dutton. He was a merchant and farmer. He was a Justice of the Peace for many years. Residence, East Bethlehem, Washington Co.

CHILDREN OF ISAAC N. AND ISABEL M. (DUTTON) CLEAVER.

1242 Salena C. Cleaver, b. 1842.   1245 Victoria L. Cleaver, b. 1849.
1243 Priscilla R. Cleaver, b. 1843. 1246 Franklin Cleaver, b. 1851.
1244 Walter D. Cleaver, b. 1846.   1247 James H. Cleaver, b. 1856.

602 Dr. Hiram T. Cleaver,[6] (John,[5] John,[4] Peter,[3] Elizabeth,[2] David,[1]), son of John and Ann (Vale) Cleaver, was born 1822, and died 1888. He married, first, Anna Hanna; second, Annie Trimble; third, Annie Garrett; and fourth, Clara Bracken. He was a physician and an instructor in the Medical College at Keokuk, Iowa.

CHILD OF DR. HIRAM T. AND ANNIE (TRIMBLE) CLEAVER.

1248 Laura M. Cleaver, b. 1850.

CHILDREN OF DR. HIRAM T. AND ANNIE (GARRETT) CLEAVER.

1249   Emma Cleaver, b. 1853.   1252   John W. Cleaver, d. 1884.
1250   Mary G. Cleaver, b. 1855.   1253   Harry Cleaver, b. 1866.
1251   Nellie Cleaver, b. 1856.

603   Hannah B. Cleaver,[6] (John,[5] John,[4] Peter,[3] Elizabeth,[2] David,[1]), daughter of John and Ann (Vale) Cleaver, was born 1824.   She married Joseph Richardson, son of John and Margaret Richardson.   Occupation, farming. Residence, Columbiana County, Ohio.

CHILDREN OF JOSEPH AND HANNAH B. (CLEAVER) RICHARDSON.

1254   Mary Etta Richardson.   1256   Anna Richardson.
1255   John C. Richardson.

604   Sheshbazzar Bentley Cleaver,[6] (John,[5] John,[4] Peter,[3] Elizabeth,[2] David,[1]), son of John and Ann (Vale) Cleaver, was born 1826.   He married Elizabeth Pyle, 1847, in Columbiana County, Ohio.   Occupation, merchant.   Residence, Wapello, Iowa.

CHILDREN OF SHESHBAZZAR B. AND ELIZABETH (PYLE) CLEAVER.

1257   Virginia Cleaver, b. 1849.   1260   John H. Cleaver, b. 1864.
1258   Mary Ada Cleaver, b. 1851.   1261   Lewretta Cleaver, b. 1866.
1259   Annie A. Cleaver, b. 1853.   1262   Hiram C. Cleaver, b. 1869.

608   John I. Cleaver,[6] (John,[5] John,[4] Peter,[3] Elizabeth,[2] David,[1]), son of John and Ann (Vale) Cleaver, was born 1834.   He married Pleasant Hill, daughter of George and Nancy (Speers) Hill, 1854.   Occupation, farmer.   Residence, East Bethlehem Township, Washington Co., Pa.

CHILDREN OF JOHN I. AND PLEASANT (HILL) CLEAVER.

1263   Mary Etta Cleaver. b. 1855; d. 1858.
1264   Joseph V. Cleaver, b. 1858.
1265   Solon H. Cleaver, b. 1861; d. 1864.
1266   Isaac N. Cleaver, b. 1865.
1267   Lestus Solon Cleaver, b. 1869. d. 1889.

624   Joseph B. Potts,[6] (John W.,[5] Jonathan,[4] David,[3] Ezekiel,[2] David,[1]), son of John W. and Elizabeth (Coyl)

Potts, was born Nov. 28, 1828, in Bedford County, Penna. He married Emily Bush, of Monroe County, Penn, in 1853. Residence, Oelwein, Fayette County, Iowa.

CHILDREN OF JOSEPH B. AND EMILY (BUSH) POTTS.

1268	Charles W. Potts.	1272	James Potts.
1269	Edwin Potts.	1273	Ella C. Potts.
1270	George C. Potts.	1274	Elizabeth Potts.
1271	John Potts.		

651 Thomas Elwood Potts,[6] (Thomas P.,[5] William,[4] William,[3] Ezekiel,[2] David,[1]), son of Thomas Pratt and Isabella (Reinhardt) Potts, was born 12 mo. 21, 1855. He married Matilda Johnson, daughter of Alexander Rodgers and Anna Louisa (———) Johnson, 1879. [For ancestry of Mrs. Potts, see "Autumn Leaves from Family Trees," page 191]. Mr. Potts is at the head of the firm of Potts & Eberle, Conveyancers, at 524 Walnut Street, Philadelphia.

CHILD OF THOMAS ELWOOD AND MATILDA (JOHNSON) POTTS.

1275 Frank Keith Potts, b. 5 mo. 28, 1880. Graduate of the Penn Charter School ; and of the University of Pennsylvania, 1900.

662 Samuel Norman,[6] (Ezekiel,[5] Anna,[4] Stephen,[3] Nathan,[2] David,[1]), son of Ezekiel and Hester (Kirk) Norman. married, 1st, Margaret VanMeter ; and 2d Emma Harker.

CHILD OF SAMUEL AND MARGARET (VANMETER) NORMAN.

1276 Mary Norman, deceased.

CHILDREN OF SAMUEL AND EMMA (HARKER) NORMAN.

1277 Mary Norman. Married and has children William and Frank.
1278 Samuel Norman.

663 Rosanna Norman,[6] (Ezekiel,[5] Anna,[4] Stephen,[3] Nathan,[2] David,[1]), daughter of Ezekiel and Hester (Kirk) Norman, married Anderson Kirk.

CHILDREN OF ANDERSON AND ROSANNA (NORMAN) KIRK.

1279	Mary Kirk.	1281	Eddie Kirk.
1280	Lydia Kirk.	1282	Emma Kirk.

671 Thomas Norman,[6] (Ezekiel,[5] Anna,[4] Stephen,[3] Nathan,[2] David,[1]), son of Ezekiel and Hester (Kirk) Norman, married Mary Weigand.

CHILDREN OF THOMAS AND MARY (WEIGAND) NORMAN.

1283 Benjamin K. Norman.	1287 Howard Norman.
1284 Elwood Norman.	1288 Charles Norman.
1285 Mary Norman.	1289 Hester Norman.
1286 William Norman.	1290 Fanny Norman.

673 William Altemus,[5] (Jane,[5] Anna,[4] Stephen,[3] Nathan,[2] David,[1]), son of Daniel ond Jane (Norman) Altemus, married Sarah Johnson.

CHILDREN OF WILLIAM AND SARAH (JOHNSON) ALTEMUS.

1291 Harry Altemus, m. Mary O'Neil.
1292 Anna Altemus, m. Leonard Haines.

1293 George Altemus.	1296 E. Channing Altemus.
1294 Ella Altemus.	1297 Wallace Altemus.

1295 Joseph Altemus.

677 Thomas N. Altemus,[6] (Jane,[5] Anna,[4] Stephen,[3] Nathan,[2] David,[1]), son of Daniel and Jane (Norman) Altemus, married Sarah Murray, daughter of Jacob Murray.

CHILDREN OF THOMAS N. AND SARAH (MURRAY) ALTEMUS.

1298 Emma Altemus, m. Irvin Zimmerman.
1299 George Altemus.

679 Morris O'Neil,[6] (Esther,[5] Anna,[4] Stephen,[3] Nathan,[2] David,[1]), son of Charles and Esther(Norman)O'Neil, married Caroline Milton.

CHILDREN OF MORRIS AND CAROLINE (MILTON) O'NEIL.

1300 Emma O'Neil, m. Cornelius H. Linton.
1301 Sarah O'Neil, m. William W. Cotter.
1302 Caroline O'Neil.
1303 Lilian O'Neil.

680 Thomas O'Neil,[6] (Esther,[5] Anna,[4] Stephen,[3] Nathan,[2] David,[1]), son of Charles and Esther(Norman) O'Neil,

71

married Elizabeth Lamon. He was a soldier in the Civil War and died from disease contracted in the service.

CHILD OF THOMAS AND ELIZABETH (LAMON) O'NEIL.

1304 Henry O'Neil.
1305 Thomas O'Neil.
1306 A. Lincoln O'Neil.
1307 Margaret O'Neil.
1308 John O'Neil.

1309 Charles O'Neil.
1310 Maurice O'Neil.
1311 William O'Neil.
1312 Esther May O'Neil.

687 Mary Norman,[6] (Stephen P.,[5] Anna,[4] Stephen,[3] Nathan,[2] David,[1]), daughter of Stephen P. and Lydia (Ottic) Norman, married Maris Taylor.

CHILDREN OF MARIS AND MARY (NORMAN) TAYLOR.

1313 Bayard Taylor.

1314 Lydia Edna Taylor.

689 Samuel Norman,[6] (Stephen P.,[5] Anna,[4] Stephen,[3] Nathan,[2] David,[1]), son of Stephen P. and Lydia (Ottic) Norman, married Mary J. Holland.

CHILDREN OF SAMUEL AND MARY J. (HOLLAND) NORMAN.

1315 John S. Norman.
1316 Clara E. Norman.
1317 Charles E. Norman.

1318 Bayard T. Norman.
1319 Samuel E. Norman.
1320 Bertha L. Norman.

691 Alice Ely,[6] (Abigail,[5] Esther,[4] Stephen,[3] Nathan,[2] David,[1]), daughter of David and Esther (Pugh) Ely, married Levi Streeper. Residence, Marble Hall, Montgomery County, Pennsylvania.

CHILDREN OF LEVI AND ALICE (ELY) STREEPER.

1321 Margaret Streeper, m. Harry Stallman.
1322 Austin Streeper.

692 Hannah Ely,[6] (Abigail,[5] Esther,[4] Stephen,[3] Nathan,[2] David,[1]), daughter of David and Abigail (Pugh) Ely, married George Davis. Residence, Marble Hall, Penna.

CHILDREN OF GEORGE AND HANNAH (ELY) DAVIS.

1323 George Davis.

1324 Anna Davis.

693 **Jonathan Ely,**[6] (Abigail,[5] Esther,[4] Stephen,[3] Nathan,[2] David,[1]), son of David and Abigail (Pugh) Ely, married Sarah Overholtzer.

CHILDREN OF JONATHAN AND SARAH (OVERHOLTZER) ELY.

1325 Kate Ely.　　1326 Alva Ely.　　1327 Burnside Ely.

694 **Hester Ely,**[6] (Abigail,[5] Esther,[4] Stephen,[3] Nathan,[2] David,[1]), daughter of David and Abigail (Pugh) Ely, married Rudolph Epright. Residence, Duncannon, Penna.

CHILDREN OF RUDOLPH AND HESTER (ELY) EPRIGHT.

1328 Mollie Epright.　　1329 Ira Epright.

696 **William Ely,**[6] (Abigail,[5] Esther,[4] Stephen,[3] Nathan,[2] David,[1]), son of David and Abigail (Pugh) Ely, married Elizabeth Lentz. Residence, Spring City, Penna.

CHILDREN OF WILLIAM AND ELIZABETH (LENTZ) ELY.

1330 Herman Ely　　1331 Maggie Ely.　　1332 Gertrude Ely.

698 **Mary E. Hendon,**[6] (Alice,[5] Esther,[4] Stephen,[3] Nathan,[2] David,[1]), daughter of James and Alice (Pugh) Hendon married Robert Forward.

CHILDREN OF ROBERT AND MARY E. (HENDON) FORWARD.

1333 John Forward.　　　1336 William Forward.
1334 Alice Forward.　　　1337 Brinton Forward.
1335 Kate Forward.

707 **Isabella Pugh,**[6] (Stephen,[5] Alice,[4] Stephen,[3] Nathan,[2] David,[1]), daughter of Stephen and Ann (Brant) Pugh, married Luke Sheard.

CHILDREN OF LUKE AND ISABELLA (PUGH) SHEARD.

1338 Winfield Scott Sheard.　　1340 Mary Sheard.
1339 Eliza Sheard, m. —— Collins.

708 **Eliza Pugh,**[6] (Stephen,[5] Esther,[4] Stephen,[3] Nathan,[2] David,[1]), daughter of Stephen and Ann (Brant) Pugh, married Thomas McDowell.

CHILDREN OF THOMAS AND ELIZA (PUGH) McDOWELL.

1341   Walter McDowell.   1343   William McDowell.
1342   Isabella McDowell.

709   **George Pugh,**[6] (Levi,[5] Esther,[4] Stephen,[3] Nathan,[2] David,[1]), son of Levi and Jane (Buchanan) Pugh, married, first, Sydney Hedman ; and second, Mary F Schmidt.

CHILDREN OF GEORGE AND SYDNEY (HEDMAN) PUGH.

1344   Mary E. Pugh.   1347   Bertha Pugh.
1345   Ella Pugh.   1348   Levi Pugh.
1346   William Pugh.

CHILDREN OF GEORGE AND MARY E. (SCHMIDT) PUGH.

1349   Mabel Pugh.   1350   Marion Pugh.

711   **Ellis Pugh,**[6] (Levi,[5] Esther,[4] Stephen,[3] Nathan,[2] David,[1]) son of Levi and Jane (Buchanan) Pugh, married Eva Gifford.   From 1872 to 1886, he was adjuster of scales in the U. S. Mint at Philadelphia.

CHILDREN OF ELLIS AND EVA (GIFFORD) PUGH.

1351   Bertha Pugh, d. y.   1353   Howard B. Pugh, d. y.
1352   Alden Pugh.   1354   Howard N. Pugh.

712   **Charles Pugh,**[6] (Levi,[5] Esther,[4] Stephen,[3] Nathan,[2] David,[1]), son of Levi and Jane (Buchanan) Pugh, married Susan Dowey.

CHILDREN OF CHARLES AND SUSAN (DOWEY) PUGH.

1355   Josephine Pugh.   1357   Alice Pugh.
1356   Robert Pugh.   1358   A child.

713   **T. Virginius Griggs,**[6] (Abigail,[5] Nathan,[4] Stephen[3] Nathan,[2] David,[1]), son of James and Abigail (Potts)Griggs, married Malinda A. Mann, 10 mo. 26, 1856.   Residence, Keokuk, Iowa.

CHILDREN OF T. VIRGINIUS AND MALINDA A. (MANN) GRIGGS.

1359   John F. Griggs, b. 4 mo. 21, 1859; m. Etta Neff.
1360   Harry L. Griggs, b. 4 mo. 2, 1862; d. 12 mo. 4, 1862.
1361   Ray V. Griggs, b. 1 mo. 18, 1866.

1362 Mary C. Griggs, b. 4 mo. 29, 1868; d. 7 mo. 9, 1869.
1363 Charles W. Griggs. b. 9 mo. 8, 1870.
1364 Perry F. Griggs, b. 2 mo. 23, 1874.
1365 Malinda A. Griggs, b. 10 mo. 29, 1883.

716 Margaret Potts,[6] (Joseph,[5] Nathan,[4] Stephen,[3] Nathan,[2] David,[1]), daughter of Joseph and Eliza (Blymyer) Potts, was born April 28, 1833, in York County, Pennsylvania. She married David R. Miller, son of Samuel and Mary (Reser) Miller, 2 mo. 21, 1858. He was born 4 mo. 9, 1825 ; and died 3 mo. 22, 1871. He was a carpenter and builder. Since the death of her husband, Mrs. Miller has resided in Harrisburg, Pennsylvania.

CHILDREN OF DAVID R. AND MARGARET (POTTS) MILLER.

1366 Morris Potts Miller, b. 12 mo. 17, 1858; d. 9 mo. 12, 1863.
1367 Ellis Potts Miller, b. 5 mo. 7, 1860; d. March 31, 1887.
1368 Herman Potts Miller, b. 12 mo. 15, 1863; m. Martha P. Jones,
1369 William Potts Miller, b. 12 mo. 22, 1865.   (997).

717 George Potts,[6] (Joseph,[5] Nathan,[4] Stephen,[3] Nathan,[2] David,[1]), son of Joseph and Eliza (Blymyer) Potts, was born Dec. 18, 1836, in York County, Pa. He married Barbara Ann Ort, 12 mo. 27, 1859. Occupation, machinist and manufacturer. Residence, Indianapolis, Indiana.

CHILDREN OF GEORGE AND BARBARA ANN (ORT) POTTS.

1370 Albert O. Potts, b. 10 mo. 6, 1860; m. Lyda Blane.
1371 J. Clayton Potts, b. 8 mo. 22, 1862.
1372 Emma J. Potts, b. 5 mo. 13, 1864.
1373 Anna E. Potts, b. 10 mo. 17. 1866.

719 Andrew B. Potts,[6] (Joseph,[5] Nathan,[4] Stephen,[3] Nathan,[2] David,[1]), son of Joseph and Eliza (Blymyer) Potts, was born Jan. 10, 1840. He married Susan Roop, daughter of Samuel Roop, 10 mo. 28, 1877. Occupation, florist. Residence, Mechanicsburg, Pennsylvania.

CHILDREN OF ANDREW B. AND SUSAN (ROOP) POTTS.

1374 William Potts, b. 3 mo. 4, 1880; d. 3 mo. 4, 1880.
1375 Andrew Potts, b. 3 mo. 1880; d. 3 mo. 16, 1880.
1376 Maud Potts, 3 mo. 10, 1880. [Adopted].

566   DAVID POTTS.

720 William C. Potts,[6] (Joseph,[5] Nathan,[4] Stephen,[3]
Nathan,[2] David,[1]), son of Joseph and Eliza (Blymyer) Potts,
was born Jan. 10, 1840, in York County, Pa.   He married,
first, Martha Thomas, 2 mo. 7, 1880.   Marriage dissolved
by divorce.   He married, second, Susan Kline, August 29,
1898.   She was born November 13, 1851.   He was formerly
a carpenter and builder, but latterly maintains a sanitarium
for the cure of invalids by massage treatment, at Mechanicsburg, Pennsylvania.

CHILDREN OF WILLIAM C. AND MARTHA (THOMAS) POTTS.

1377   Ross R. Potts, b. 10 mo. 19, 1880.
1378   Florence Potts, b. March 25, 1889.

721 Joseph Rankin Potts,[6] (Joseph,[5] Nathan,[4] Stephen,[3] Nathan,[2] David,[1]), son of Joseph and Eliza (Blymyer) Potts, was born January 19, 1843, in York County, Pa.
He married Malinda Ross, 10 mo. 25, 1868.   Occupation,
machinist.   Residence. Mechanicsburg, Pennsylvania.

CHILDREN OF JOSEPH R. AND MALINDA (ROSS) POTTS.

1379   Berva Potts, b. 11 mo. 20, 1872; m. John G. Way, 1898.
1380   Alletta M. Potts, b. 5 mo. 22, 1876; d. August 23, 1892.
1381   Minnie E. Potts, b. 1 mo. 12, 1879.

725 Anna Potts,[6] (William[5] Nathan,[4] Stephen,[3] Na-
than,[2] David,[1]), daughter of William and Lanah (Kunkle)
Potts, was born Dec. 8, 1842.   She married Martin Laird.
Occupation, farmer.   Residence, Lewisberry, Penna.

CHILDREN OF MARTIN AND ANNA (POTTS) LAIRD.

1382   M. Lily Laird.   1383   E. Jane Laird.   1384   Herman Laird.

726 William K. Potts,[6] (William,[5] Nathan,[4] Stephen.[3]
Nathan,[2] David,[1]), son of William and Lanah (Kunkle)
Potts, was born Oct. 11, 1845, in York County, Pennsylva-
nia.   He married Anna Getz.   Residence, Plum Creek, Neb.

CHILD OF WILLIAM K. AND ANNA (GETZ) POTTS.

1385   Marlin J. Potts.

729 Penrose L. Potts,[6] (William,[5] Nathan,[4] Stephen,[3] Nathan,[2] David,[1]), son of William and Lanah (Kunkle) Potts, was born March 26, 1853, in York County, Pa. He married Anna Huey. Residence, Plum Creek, Neb.

CHILDREN OF PENROSE L. AND ANNA (HUEY) POTTS.

1386 Bessie H. Potts.   1387 Clista H. Potts.

732 Ann Potts,[6] (George,[5] Nathan,[4] Stephen,[3] Nathan,[2] David,[1]), daughter of George and Mary (Watts) Potts, was born 3 mo. 9, 1833, and died 3 mo. 9, 1877. She married Henry Reigel. Residence, Harrisburg, Pennsylvania.

CHILDREN OF HENRY AND ANN (POTTS) REIGEL.

1388 Hanson S. Reigel, b. 11 mo. 7, 1856; m. Alwilda Fry.
1389 Elmer Reigel, b. 1 mo. 2, 1859; d. 8 mo. 18, 1860
1390 Alice M. Reigel, b. 11 mo. —, 1861; m. Abner Forrest.
1391 Sherman Reigel, b. 8 mo. 1, 1866.
1392 William Adam Reigel, b. 7 mo. 5, 1868.

733 Harriet Potts,[6] (George,[5] Nathan,[4] Stephen,[3] Nathan,[2] David,[1]), daughter of George and Mary (Watts) Potts, was born 10 mo. 21, 1834, and died 12 mo. 25, 1862. She married Thomas Grier, 1860. He died 1866.

CHILD OF THOMAS AND HARRIET (POTTS) GRIER.

1393 Charles Grier, b. July —; 1861.

734 Elmira J. Potts,[6] (George,[5] Nathan,[4] Stephen,[3] Nathan,[2] David,[1]), daughter of George and Mary (Watts) Potts, was born 5 mo. 22, 1836. She married Joseph Wells, 1859. Occupation, grocer. Residence, Harrisburg, Penn.

CHILDREN OF JOSEPH AND ELMIRA J. (POTTS) WELLS.

1394 Mary E. Wells, m. Jacob Sourbeer.
1395 Ida Wells.   1398 Viola Wells.
1396 Minerva Wells.   1399 Clara Wells.
1397 Morris T. Weits.   1400 Harriet Wells.

735 Susanna Potts,[6] (George,[5] Nathan,[4] Stephen,[3] Nathan,[2] David,[1]), daughter of George and Mary (Watts)

Potts, was born 9 mo. 10, 1838. She married William Makibben. Occupation, machinist. Residence, Harrisburg, Pennsylvania.

CHILDREN OF WILLIAM AND SUSANNA (POTTS) MAKIBBEN.

1401 James G. Makibben, b. 12 mo. 6, 1858; m. Phebe Sourbeer.
1402 Alva C. Makibben, d. 7 mo. 8, 1860.
1403 Horatio Ross Makibben, b. 8 mo. 3, 1862; d. 7 mo. 2, 1863.
1404 Robert T. Makibben, b. 9 mo. 22, 1864.
1405 Anna L. Makibben, b. 4 mo. 22, 1868.
1426 Charles T. Makibben, b. 4 mo. 29, 1871.
1407 Rolland J. Makibben, k. 6 mo. 19, 1874.
1408 Bessie L. Makibben, b. 5 mo. 4, 1878.

736 Andrew W. Potts,[6] (George,[5] Nathan,[4] Stephen,[3] Nathan,[2] David,[1]), son of George and Mary (Watts) Potts, was born 8 mo. 28, 1840. He married Jane Ely, (695). Occupation, baker. Residence, William Penn, Penna.

CHILDREN OF ANDREW W. AND JANE (ELY) POTTS.

1409 M. Abbie Potts.   1410 Emma Potts.

737 Eliza Potts,[6] (George,[5] Nathan,[4] Stephen,[3] Nathan,[2] David,[1]), daughter of George and Mary (Watts) Potts, was born 2 mo. 2, 1842. She married David Black, 5 mo. 19, 1864. He was born 5 mo. —, 1835.

CHILDREN OF DAVID AND ELIZA (POTTS) BLACK.

1411 William C. Black, b. 12 mo. 13, 1865; d. 5 mo. 12, 1871.
1412 George L. Black, b. 8 mo. 4, 1867; d. 5 mo. 7, 1871.
1413 Sarah S. Black, b. 2 mo. 10, 1869; d, 5 mo. 16, 1871.
1414 Clinton Black, b. 11 mo. 15, 1870; 4 mo. 16, 1872.
1415 Charles N. Black, b. 1 mo. 17, 1874,

739 Milton G. Potts,[6] (George,[5] Nathan,[4] Stephen,[3] Nathan,[2] David,[1]), son of George and Mary (Watts) Potts, was born 1 mo. 25, 1845. He married Ella Ringler, 4 mo. 14, 1867.

CHILDREN OF MILTON G. AND ELLA (RINGLER) POTTS.

1416 George C. Potts.   1418 Ellen Alwilda Potts.
1417 Emily Elizabeth Potts.

MILTON G. POTTS.   .   GEORGE C. POTTS.
PAGE 508.

740 Ann Powell,[6] (Jane,[5] Nathan,[4] Stephen,[3] Nathan,[2] David,[1]), daughter of Jacob and Jane (Potts) Powell, was born 11 mo. 1, 1830. She married Elijah Crone, 1859.

CHILDREN OF ELIJAH AND ANN (POTTS) CRONE.

1419 Bartlet Crone, m. Sarah Boring.
1420 Andrew Crone, m. Mary Ortmyer.
1421 A daughter.   1423 George Crone.
1422 Norris Crone.   1424 Harvey Crone.

741 Harriet Powell,[6] (Jane,[5] Nathan,[4] Stephen,[3] Nathan,[2] David,[1]), daughter of Jacob and Jane (Potts) Powell, was born 12 mo. 2, 1832. She married Jonathan Griest, 12 mo. 13, 1855. Occupation, painter. Residence, Lewisberry, York County, Pennsylvania.

CHILDREN OF JONATHAN AND HARRIET (POWELL) GRIEST.

1425 Earnest Griest, b. 11 mo. 26, 1856.
1426 Alice M. Griest, b. 3 mo. 14, 1858; m. Robert Stonecipher.
1427 William P. Griest, b. 3 mo. 15, 1860.

744 Abram Powell,[6] (Jane,[5] Nathan,[4] Stephen,[3] Nathan,[2] David,[1]), son of Jacob and Jane (Potts) Powell, was born 4 mo. 23, 1838. He married, first, Caroline Herman, 12 mo. 11, 1862. He married, second, Susan Beard.

CHILDREN OF ABRAM AND CAROLINE (HERMAN) POWELL.

1428 Charles Powell.   1431 Edward Powell.
1428 Grant Powell.   1432 Levi Powell.
1430 Mary Powell.   1433 George Powell.

745 Andrew S. Powell,[6] (Jane,[5] Nathan,[4] Stephen,[3] Nathan,[2] David,[1]), son of Jacob and Jane (Potts) Powell, was born 12 mo, 11, 1839. He married Elizabeth Shanley, 7 mo. 23, 1871.

CHILDREN OF ANDREW S. AND ELIZABETH (SHANLEY) POWELL.

1434 Viola Powell.   1435 Ray Powell.

746 George F. Powell, M. D.,[6] (Jane,[5] Nathan,[4] Stephen,[3] Nathan,[2] David,[1]), son of Jacob and Jane (Potts)

72

Powell, was born 4 mo, 23, 1843. He married Mary C. Ensminger 11 mo. 21, 1872. She was born 4 mo. 11, 1851. Residence, Burnside, Clearfield County, Pennsylvania.

CHILDREN OF DR. GEORGE F. AND MARY C. (ENSMINEER) POWELL.

1436   Beulah Powell, b. 9 mo. 12, 1873; d. 9 mo. 7, 1880.
1437   Fanny P. Powell, b. 8 mo. 4, 1877.
1438   Max E. Powell, b. 3 mo. 10, 1882.

747   Jacob A. Powell,[6] (Jane,[5] Nathan,[4] Stephen,[3] Nathan,[2] David,[1]), son of Jacob and Jane (Potts) Powell, was born 2 mo. 1, 1847.   He married Sarah Miller 7, 23, 1871.

CHILDREN OF JACOB A. AND SARAH (MILLER) POWELL.

1439   Frank Powell.   1442   Robert Powell.
1440   Bertha Powell.   1443   Emma Powell.
1441   Albert Powell.

750   Wellington Jones,[6] (William,[5] Alice,[4] Stephen,[3] Nathan,[2] David,[1]), son of Willian and Sarah (Ansby) Jones, married ——— ———.   Occupation, printer.   Residence, Philadelphia.

CHILDREN OF WELLINTON AND ——— (———) JONES.

1444   William Jones.   And others.

752   Elizabeth Jones,[6] (George,[5] Alice,[4] Stephen,[3] Nathan,[2] David,[1]), daughter of George and Joan (Stager) Jones, married Dr. Charles Cressler.   Residence, Chambersburg, Pennsylvania.

CHILDREN OF DR. CHARLES AND ELIZABETH (JONES) CRESSLER.

1445   Elva Cressler.   1448   Belle Cressler.
1446   Emily Cressler.   1449   Alice Cressler.
1447   Florence Cressler.   1450   Nellie Cressler.

765   Caroline L. Potts,[6] (Percival M.,[5] Nathan R.,[4] Nathan,[3] Nathan,[2] David,[1]), daughter of Percival Morgan and Laura Louisa (Cauffman) Potts, married Thomas J. Wentworth.   Residence, Baltimore, Maryland.

CHILDREN OF THOMAS J. AND CAROLINE L. (POTTS) WENTWORTH.

1451   Stanley Wentworth.   1452   Adele Wentworth.

Capt. H. W. Shipley —
91st Regt. PV.
1891

CAPTAIN HOWARD WHEATLEY SHIPLEY.
PAGE 570 1-2.

771 **Capt. Howard Wheatley Shipley,[6]** (Elenora,[5] Nathan R.,[4] Nathan,[3] Nathan,[2] David,[1]), son of Augustus B. and Elenora (Potts) Shipley, was born in 1845. At the age of sixteen, he enlisted in Company I, —— Regiment of the Pennsylvania Infantry, April 30, 1861, which moved to Chambersburg and was assigned to the Third Brigade, First Division of Patterson's Army, on June 30, 1861. Invaded Virginia July 2, and moved to the support of troops engaged at Falling Waters and the operations of the Shenandoah. He was mustered out August 6, 1861, and at once re-enlisted as Second Lieutenant in Company G, Ninty-First Regiment Pennsylvania Volunteer Infantry, and attached to the Fifth Army Corps. He was promoted to First Lieutenant and Acting Adjutant of the Regiment, December 2, 1861, and to Captain on May 12, 1864. He was wounded at the Battle of Spotsylvania Court House on May 12, 1864, and mustered out December 2, 1864, at the expiration of term of service.

His active services included the following: Duty in defence of Washington, D. C., and at Alexandria, Virginia until August; engaged at Antietam, September 17, 18, 1862; Action near Shepardstown, September 19, 20; Action near same place, October 15, 16; Battle of Fredericksburg; Assault on Fredericksburg Heights; Action at the Block House; Battle of Chancelorsville; Battle of Gettysburg; Actions at Antietam Creek; Engagement at Bristol Station, Virginia; Engagement at Rappahannock Station; Battles of the Wilderness, Virginia; Parker's Store; About Spottsylvania; Plank Road; Laural Hill; Bloody Angle; Myers' House; Totopotamy Creek; Hanover Town; Battle of Cold Harbor; Bethsaida Church; Allen's Mills; Action at White Oak Swamp; Siege of Petersburg; Assault on Suffolk and Petersburg Railroad; Jerusalem Plank Road; Mine Exposion; Weldon Railroad; Battle of Poplar Springs Church; Engagement at Dawes' House; and Hatcher's Run. He died October 10, 1895. [See portrait].

776 Charles Sower Potts, M. D.,[6] (Francis C.,[5] Nathan R.,[4] Nathan,[3] Nathan,[2] David,[1]), son of Francis C. and Emma (Bilger) Potts, was born January 30, 1864. He graduated from the Central High School of Philadelphia in 1882, and from the Medical Department of the University of Pennsylvania in 1885. While a student in the University, he took part in athletics, and in 1884 and 1885, rowed in the "Varsity Eight." After graduation he served as Interne in the Philadelphia and University Hospitals and the State Hospital for the insane at Norristown, Penna. He is Instructor in Nervous Diseases and Electro-Therapeutics in the University of Pennsylvania ; Assistant Neurologist to the University Hospital ; Neurologist to the Philadelphia Hospital ; Consulting Alienist to the State Penitentiary for the Eastern District of Pennsylvania ; Consulting Physician to the Hospital for the Insane of Atlantic County, New Jersey ; Fellow of the College of Physicians of Philadelphia ; First Vice President of the Philadelphia Neurological Society, for 1901 ; Member of the American Medical Association ; Member of the Philadelphia County Medical Society ; etc.; Author of Manual of Nervous and Mental Diseases, for Practitioners and Students. Residence, Philadelphia.

772 **Malcolm Augustus Shipley,**[6] (Eleanor,[5] Nathan R.,[4] Nathan,[3] Nathan,[2] David,[1]), son of Augustus B. and Eleanor (Potts) Shipley, married Josephine Gregg.

CHILDREN OF MALCOLM A. AND JOSEPHINE (GREGG) SHIPLEY.

1453 Mary E. Shipley.   1455 Malcolm A. Shipley.
1454 Lily Shipley.   1456 Arthur C. Shipley.

783 **Elizabeth Keesey,**[6] (Alice,[5] Esther,[4] Alice,[3] Nathan,[2] David,[1]), daughter of John and Alice (Colley) Keesey, married Thornton Fleming Hickey. Both are deceased. Mr. Hickey was a builder and contractor and did a prosperous business, but lost heavily by fire in California.

CHILDREN OF THORNTON F. AND ELIZABETH (KEESEY(HICKEY.

1457 David Clinton Hickey. Died a prisoner of war at Andersonville.
1458 Mary Ellen Hickey, deceased.
1459 Emma Catharine Hickey, m. Louis Beach.
1460 Susanna G. Hickey. A teacher at Washington, D. C.

785 **Jacob Childs,**[6] (Ann T.,[5] Mary,[4] Alice,[3] Nathan,[2] David,[1]), son of Jacob and Ann Thomas (Moore) Childs, was born — —, ——; and died 3 mo. –, 1886. He married Lydia ———.

CHILDREN OF JACOB AND LYDIA (———) CHILDS.

1461 Louis M. Childs. An attorney at law, of Norristown, Penna.
1462 Mary Childs.   1464 Emma Childs.
1463 Walter Childs.   1465 Lilian Childs.

787 **Abram Kane,**[6] (Elizabeth T.,[5] Mary,[4] Alice,[3] Nathan,[2] David,[1]), son of Abram and Elizabeth T. (Moore) Kane, married Charlotte McVaughn.

CHILDREN OF ABRAM AND CHARLOTTE (McVAUGHN) KANE.

1466 Martha Kane, m. Charles Spencer.
1467 Sarah Kane.   1468 Louisa Kane.   1469 Mary Kane.

788 **Lewis V. Moore,**[6] (Alexander,[5] Mary,[4] Alice,[3] Nathan,[2] David,[1]), son of Alexander and Harriet (Deitz) Moore, was born ——; and died 4 mo. —, 1886. He marred E. Jane Phillips.

1470   Alice Moore, m. ——— ———.   Residence, Pottsville, Pa.

789   Issacher Peterman,[6] (Jacob,[5] Priscilla,[4] Alice,[3] Nathan,[2] David,[1]), son of Jacob and Mary (Engard) Peterman, married Miriam Fox.

CHILDREN OF ISSACHER AND MIRIAM (FOX) PETERMAN.
1471   Margaret Elizabeth Peterman, m. William E. Crissey.
1472   Jacob Peterman, m. Elizabeth Zellner.
1473   Emma S. Peterman, m. Thomas Pilson.
1474   Ellen P. Peterman, m. John Little.
1475   Maria L. Peterman.
1476   Miriam K. Peterman, m. Charles Clark.
1477   Caroline Peterman, deceased.
1478   Anna H. Peterman.

792   John E. Peterman,[6] (Jacob,[5] Priscilla,[4] Alice,[3] Nathan,[2] David,[1]), son of Jacob and Mary (Engard) Peterman, married Mary West.

CHILDREN OF JOHN E. AND MARY (WEST) PETERMAN.
1479   Clara Peterman, m. William Chester.

794   Benjamin F. Peterman,[6] (Jacob,[5] Priscilla,[4] Alice,[3] Nathan,[2] David,[1]), son of Jacob and Mary (Engard) Peterman, married Anna Harris.

CHILDREN OF BENJAMIN AND ANNA (HARRIS) PETERMAN.
1480   William H. Peterman.

798   Matilda M. Ramsay,[6] (Ann,[5] Priscilla,[4] Alice,[3] Nathan,[2] David,[1]), daughter of Alexander and Ann (Peterman) Ramsay, married Jacob Vaughn.

CHILDREN OF JACOB AND MATILDA M. (RAMSAY) VAUGHN.
1481   John A. Vaughn, deceased.
1482   Horace B. Vaughn, m. Mary ———.
1483   Jacob K. Vaughn, m.
1484   Matilda M. Vaughn.
1485   Anna Vaughn, m. John Hines.
1486   Caroline Vaughn, m. Samuel Dyer.

1487 Emma Vaughn, m. William Harvey.
1488 John Vaughn.

800 Maria Ramsay,⁶ (Ann,⁵ Priscilla,⁴ Alice,³ Nathan,²
David,¹), daughter of Alexander and Ann (Peterman)
Ramsay, married John Weik.

> Children of John and Maria (Ramsay) Weik

1489 Louisa Weik, m. Dr. William Bell.
1490 Anna M. Weik.   1491 John Weik.

801 Caroline A. Ramsay,⁶ (Ann,⁵ Priscilla,⁴ Alice,³
Nathan,² David,¹), daughter of Alexander and Ann (Peterman) Ramsay, married L. N. Brognard.

> Children of L. N. and Caroline A. (Ramsay) Brognard.

1492 Henry H. Brognard, m. Mary ———.
1493 G. Curtis Brognard, d. unm.
1494 Caroline Brognard, m. Dr. ——— Buchanan.
1495 Anna K. Brognard.

803 Ellen Peterman,⁶ (Benjamin F.⁵ Priscilla,⁴ Alice,³
Nathan,² David,¹), daughter of Benjamin F. and Mary
(Murray) Peterman, married, first, ——— Preston ; and
second, ——— Lukens.

> Child of ——— and Ellen (Peterman) Lukens.

1496 Alden Lukens.

804 Joseph Peterman,⁶ (Benjamin F.,⁵ Priscilla,⁴ Alice³
Nathan,² David,¹), son of Benjamin F. and Mary (Murray)
Peterman, married Kate ———.

> Children of Joseph and Kate (———) Peterman.

1497 Benjamin Peterman.   1499 Esther Peterman.
1498 Joseph Peterman.   1500 ——— Peterman.

805 Maria Peterman,⁶ (Benjamin F.,⁵ Priscilla,⁴ Alice,³
Nathan,² David,¹), daughter of Benjamin F. and Mary
(Murray) Peterman, married John Harris.

CHILD OF JOHN AND MARIA (PETERMAN) HARRIS.

1501   Kate Harris, m. ——— Wentz.

810   Hester Peterman,[6] (Benjamin F.,[5] Priscilla,[4] Alice,[3] Nathan,[2] David,[1]), daughter of Benjamin F. and Mary (Murray) Peterman, married John Wood.   ·

CHILDREN OF JOHN AND HESTER (PETERMAN) WOOD.

1502   Mary Peterman.   And others.

813   Priscilla Lukens,[6] (Esther,[5] Priscilla,[4] Alice,[3] Nathan,[2] David,[1]), daughter of Clayton and Esther (Peterman) Lukens, married, first, John Stemple ; and second, ——— Shallenberger.

CHILDREN OF JOHN AND PRISCILLA (LUKENS) STEMPLE.

1503   George Stemple.   1504   Ann Stemple.

CHILD OF ——— AND PRISCILLA (LUKENS) SHALLENBERGER.

1505   Walter Shellenberger, m. Bertha Lauderbaugh.

814   Allen Lukens,[6] (Esther,[5] Priscilla,[4] Alice,[3] Nathan,[2] David,[1]), son of Clayton and Esther (Peterman) Lukens, married Mary Butcher.

CHILDREN OF ALLEN AND MARY (BUTCHER) LUKENS.

1506   Mary Lukens, m. ——— Zimmerman.
1507   Esther Lukens.
1508   Reeves Lukens.

816   Thomas Lukens,[6] (Esther,[5] Priscilla,[4] Alice,[3] Nathan,[2] David,[1]), son of Clayton and Esther (Peterman) Lukens, married Mary ———.

CHILDREN OF THOMAS AND MARY (———) LUKENS.

1509   Elwood Lukens.   1510   Mary Lukens.

818   Harriet A. White,[6] (Maria,[5] Priscilla,[4] Alice,[3] Nathan,[2] David,[1]), daughter of John and Maria (Peterman) White, married Henry Rodenberg.

CHILDREN OF HENRY AND HARRIET A. (WHITE) RODENBERG.

1511 Albert Rodenberg.　　　1514 Anna M. Rodenberg.
1512 Mary T. Rodenberg.　　　1515 Harriet A. Rodenberg.
1513 Henry Rodenberg.　　　　1516 Kate Rodenberg.

819　**Anna M. White,**[6] (Maria,[5] Priscilla,[4] Alice,[3] Nathan,[2] David,[1]), daughter of John and Maria (Peterman) White, married James Smeeton.

CHILDREN OF JAMES AND ANNA M. (WHITE) SMEETON.

1517 Harriet A. Smeeton.　　　1520 N. Brognard Smeeton.
1518 Maria Theresa Smeeton.　　1521 Mary Smeeton.
1519 Annie Smeeton.　　　　　1522 Susan Smeeton.

820　**Evan Henry Everman,**[6] (Alice,[5] Esther,[4] Alice,[3] Nathan,[2] David,[1]), son of William H. and Alice (Peterman) Everman, married Maria Gideon.

CHILDREN OF EVAN H. AND MARIA (GIDEON) EVERMAN.

1523 Alice P. Everman.　　　　1525 Ellie Everman.
1524 Mary Everman.

821　**George W. Everman,**[6] (Alice,[5] Priscilla,[4] Alice,[3] Nathan,[2] David,[1]), son of William H. and Alice (Peterman) Everman, married Edith T. Everman.

CHILDREN OF GEORGE W. AND EDITH T. (BENNETT) EVERMAN.

1526　Caroline B. Everman.
1527　Anna Maria Everman, m. George Reeves.
1528　Alice P. Everman, m. —— Clinton.
1529　Joseph B. Everman.
1530　Sarah B. Everman, m. Isaac Elliott.
1531　John W. Everman.

823　**Anna Maria Everman,**[6] (Alice,[5] Priscilla,[4] Alice,[3] Nathan,[2] David,[1]), daughter of William H. and Alice (Peterman) Everman, married Thomas Robert Petty.

CHILDREN OF THOMAS R. AND ANNA M. (EVERMAN) PETTY.

1532　Alice G. Petty, m. William Bucklin.
1533　Edtth B. Petty, m. Salm Hudson.
1534　Robert W. Petty.

1535 Annie Petty.
1536 Grace Petty.
1537 Lydia Petty.

1538 Lydia Petty.
1539 Melinda Petty.
1540 William Petty.

826 Matilda V. Peterman,[6] (Joseph,[5] Priscilla,[4] Alice,[3] Nathan,[2] David,[1]), daughter of Joseph and Eliza (Roberts) Peterman, married Levi Cutler.

CHILD OF LEVI AND MATILDA V. (PETERMAN) CUTLER.

1541 Edith Cutler, m. Edwin Stokes.

828 Benjamin Hallowell,[6] (Job,[5] Hannah,[4] Alice,[3] Nathan,[2] David,[1]), son of Job and Hannah (Robinson) Hallowell, married Rebecca Whitney.

CHILD OF BENJAMIN AND REBECCA (WHITNEY) HALLOWELL.

1542 Harry Hallowell, m. Mary ———.

831 Rebecca M. Tyson,[6] (Mary R.,[5] Hannah,[4] Alice,[3] Nathan,[2] David,[1]), daughter of William and Mary R. (Hallowell) Tyson, was born 11 mo. 11, 1824. She married John B. Otto.

CHILDREN OF JOHN B. AND REBECCA M. (TYSON) OTTO.

1543 Emily T. Otto, m. Fred W. Swartz.
1544 Ella W. Otto, m. Lewis P. Lauger.
1545 Harry R. Otto, m. Jennie Garwood.
1546 Mary T. Otto.
1547 Martha P. Otto.

833 Ira C. Tyson,[6] (Mary R.,[5] Hannah,[4] Alice,[3] Nathan,[2] David,[1]), son of William and Mary R. (Hallowell) Tyson, was born 3 mo. 3, 1830 He married, first, Fannie L. Hunt. No issue. He married, second, Hettie Sperling.

CHILDREN OF IRA C. AND HETTIE (SPRLING) TYSON.

1548 Edward R. Tyson.
1549 Louis L. Tyson.
1550 Fannie Tyson.
1551 Mary Tyson.
1552 Charles W. Tyson.

834 Job H. Tyson,[6] (Mary R.,[5] Hannah,[4] Alice,[3] Nathan,[2] David,[1]), son of William and Mary P., (Hallowell)

Tyson, was born 10 mo. 27, 1833. He married Isabella Miller.

CHILDREN OF JOB H. AND ISABELLA (MILLER) TYSON.

1553 James M. Tyson. 1554 William B. Tyson.

836 Morris Tyson,[6] (Mary R.,[5] Hannah,[4] Alice,[3] Nathan,[2] David,[1]), son of William and Mary R. (Hallowell) Tyson, married Zilpha Ammon.

CHILDREN OF MORRIS AND ZILPHA (AMMON) TYSON.

1555 Warrenne L. Tyson. 1556 Raymond Tyson.

839 Thomas Smith,[6] (Zebulon,[5] Martha,[4] Alice,[3] Nathan,[2] David,[1]), son of Zebulon and Hannah (Huston) Smith, married Hannah ———.

CHILDREN OF THOMAS AND HANNAH (———) SMITH.

1557 Zebulon Smith. 1559 Thomas Smith.
1558 Susanna Smith. 1560 William Smith.

840 Edmund Smith,[6] (Zebulon,[5] Martha,[4] Alice,[3] Nathan,[2] David,[1]), son of Zebulon and Hannah (Huston) Smith, married Rebecca J. Adamson.

CHILDREN OF EDMUND AND REBECCA J. (ADAMSON) SMITH.

1561 Elizabeth A. Smith. 1562 Hannah K. Smith.

843 William Smith,[6] (James,[5] Martha,[4] Alice,[3] Nathan,[2] David,[1]), son of James and Esther (Brooks) Smith, married Mary Rickert.

CHILDREN OF WILLIAM AND MARY (RICKERT) SMITH.

1563 Martha Smith. 1564 Laura Smith.

844 James Smith,[6] (James,[5] Martha,[5] Alice,[3] Nathan,[2] David,[1]), son of James and Esther (Brooks) Smith, married

CHILD OF JAMES AND ——— (———) SMITH.

1565 Maud Smith.

73

845 Alice Smith,⁶ (James,⁵ Martha,,⁴ Alice,³ Nathan,² David,¹), daughter of James and Esther (Brooks) Smith, married Daniel Kirkner.

CHILDREN OF DANIEL AND ALICE (SMITH) KIRKNER.
1566 Lizzie Kirkner.   1567 Joseph Kirkner.

846 Ida Smith,⁶ (James,⁵ Martha,⁴ Alice,³ Nathan,² David,¹), daughter of James and Esther (Brooks) Smith, married William McDowell.

CHILD OF WILLIAM AND IDA (SMITH) McDOWELL.
1568 Susan McDowell.

848 Elizabeth Smith,⁶ (William J.,⁵ Martha,⁴ Alice,³ Nathan,² David,¹), daughter of William J. and Sarah (Sheetz) Smith, married Edward Davenport.

CHILD OF EDWARD AND ELIZABETH (SMITH) DAVENPORT.
1569 William Davenport.

850 Emily Smith,⁶ (William J.,⁵ Martha,⁴ Alice,³ Nathan,² David.¹), daughter of William J. and Sarah (Sheetz) Smith, married John Mitchell.

CHILD OF JOHN AND EMILY (SMITH) MITCHELL.
1570 William Mitchell.

851 William J. Smith,⁶ (William J.,⁵ Martha,⁴ Alice,³ Nathan,² David,¹), son of William J. and Sarah (Sheetz) Smith, married Amanda Brook.

CHILDREN OF WILLIAM J. AND AMANDA (BROOK) SMITH.
1571 Isaac B. Smith.   1572 Emily M. Smith.

854 Charles H. Smith,⁶ (Christopher H.,⁵ Martha,⁴ Alice,³ Nathan,² David,¹), son of Christopher H. and Mary W. (Freas) Smith, married Harriet Johnson.

CHILDREN OF CHARLES H. AND HARRIET (JOHNSON) SMITH.
1573 Mary Smith.   1574 Alice Smith.

855 Sanford Clay Smith,[6] (Christopher H.,[5] Martha,[4] Alice,[3] Nathan,[2] David,[1]), son of Christopher H. and Mary W. (Freas) Smith, married Theresa Austin.

CHILD OF SANFORD C. AND THERESA (AUSTIN) SMITH.

1575 Florence Smith.

863 Comley Sanford Smith,[6] (Job H.,[5] Martha,[4] Alice,[3] Nathan,[2] David,[1]), son of Job H. and Margaret (Hinkle) Smith, married Josephine White.

CHILDREN OF COMLEY S. AND JOSEPHINE (WHITE) SMITH.

1576 Isabella Smith.
1577 Anna Bertha Smith.

1578 H. Margaret Smith.
1579 Alice W. Smith.

865 Alice M. Smith,[6] (Job H.,[5] Martha,[4] Alice,[3] Nathan,[2] David,[1]), daughter of Job H. and Mary V. (Dark) Smith, married John Hughes.

CHILD OF JOHN AND ALICE M. (SMITH) HUGHES.

1580 Henry S. Hughes, b. 1886.

868 Mary Emma Smith,[6] (Henry,[5] Martha,[4] Alice,[3] Nathan,[2] David,[1]), daughter of Henry and Margaret(Sheetz) Smith, married George Barnes.

CHILDREN OF GEORGE AND MARY E. (SMITH) BARNES.

1581 Harry Barnes.
1582 Mary Barnes.
1583 William Barnes.

1584 Emma Barnes.
1585 Alice Barnes.

877 Barclay Thomas,[6] (Jarrett,[5] Ann,[4] Zebulon,[3] Nathan,[2] David,[1]) son of Jarrett and Catharine (Schimmerhorn) Thomas, married —— ——.

CHILDREN OF BARCLAY AND —— (——) THOMAS.

1586 Ann Thomas.
1587 Emma Thomas.

880 Martha Thomas,[6] (William,[5] Ann,[4] Zebulon,[3] Nathan,[2] David,[1]), daughter of William and Sarah (Farringer) Thomas, was born August 31, 1832. She married William H. Yerkes.

CHILDREN OF WILLIAM H. AND MARTHA (THOMAS) YERKES.

1588 Frank Yerkes, b. November 7, 1859; d. March 14, 1874.
1589 Carrie Yerkes, b. June 27, 1861; m. Howard Mather.

881 Mary Thomas,[6] (William,[5] Ann,[4] Zebulon,[3] Nathan,[2] David,[1]), daughter of William and Susan (Farringer) Thomas, was born Mar. 13, 1834. She married George Hart, son of Jacob and Hannah (Zeiber) Hart, February 26, 1857. He was born December 5, 1828.

CHILDREN OF GEORGE AND MARY (THOMAS) HART.

1590 Andrew Calvin Hart, b. March 1, 1858.
1591 Marshall T. Hart, b. June 5, 1860.
1592 Raymond P. Hart, b. Jannary 14, 1862; d. March 27, 1887.
1593 James H. Hart, b. April 24, 1864.
1594 Arvilla Hart, b. May 9, 1866.
1595 George L. Hart, b. June 22, 1868.
1596 Mary A. Hart, b. December 26, 1871; d. April 24, 1889.
1597 Philip B. Hart, b. July 20, 1874.

882 Seth Thomas,[6] (William,[5] Ann,[4] Zebulon,[3] Nathan,[2] David,[1]), son of William and Susan (Farringer) Thomas, was born Jan. 1, 1836, He married Mary Bates.

CHILDREN OF SETH AND MARY (BATES) THOMAS.

1598 Hepzibah Thomas.	1602 Joseph Thomas.
1599 Ella Jane Thomas.	1603 Alexander Thomas.
1600 George Thomas.	1604 Barclay Thomas.
1601 Cora Thomas.	

884 Harry H. Thomas,[6] (William,[5] Ann,[4] Zebulon,[3] Nathan,[2] David,[1]), son of William and Susan (Farringer) Thomas, was born January 26, 1840. He married Abigail Fisher, daughter of George Fisher.

CHILD OF HARRY H. AND ABIGAIL (FISHER) THOMAS.

1605 Anna P. Thomas.

885 Anna Thomas,[6] (Jonathan,[5] Ann,[4] Zebulon,[3] Nathan,[2] David,[1]), daughter of Jonathan and Hannah (Roberts) Thomas, was born 3 mo. 6, 1834. She married Dr. J. K. Piersol, a physician. Residence, Adrian, Michigan.

Children of Dr. J. K. and Anna (Thomas) Piersol.

1606 Harry Angell Piersol.   1608 Frances B. Piersol.
1607 Mabel Piersol.

890 **Mary Thomas,**[6] (Jonathan,[5] Ann,[4] Zebulon,[3] Nathan,[2] David,[1]), daughter of Jonathan and Hannah (Roberts) Thomas, was born May 13, 1843, and died February 15, 1879. She married Henry Carson, of Hartford, Conn. He enlisted in the 71st Regiment, Penusylvania Volunteers, at the opening of the Civil War, as a Second Lieutenant and rose to a Captain. Being wounded, he was dicharged from service in 1863.

Children of Henry and Mary (Thomas) Carson.

1609 William Corson Carson, b. May —, 1864; d. March 16, 1866.
1610 Lewis Reid Carson, b. April 28, 1867.
1611 Rev. Harry Roberts Carson, b. Dec. 8, 1869. He is a Minister of the Gospel in the Protestant Episcopal Church.
1612 Charles Colfax Carson, b. March 31, 1872.
1613 Albert Warren Carson, b. July 13, 1874.
1614 Frank Thomas Carson, b. June 8, 1877.

892 **Martha Thomas,**[6] (Jonathan,[5] Ann,[4] Zebulon,[3] Nathan,[2] David,[1]), daughter of Jonathan and Hannah (Roberts) Thomas, was born 8 mo. 10, 1848. She married J. Ross Lake, son of Jacob and Sarah Lake.

Children of Ross and Martha (Thomas) Lake.

1615 Emily Thomas Lake, b. March 18, 1882.

901 **Alice Hallowell,**[6] (William,[5] Alice,[4] Zebulon,[3] Nathan,[2] David,[1]), daughter of William and Deborah (Worrell) Hallowell, was born 2 mo. 11, 1832. She married Isaac Wayne Holstein, son of George W. and Elizabeth (Wayne) Holstein, 12 mo. 27, 1854. He was born 1 mo. 25, 1823, and died April 8, 1884. Residence, Bridgeport, Montgomery County, Pennsylvania.

Children of Isaac W. and Alice (Hallowell) Holstein.

1616 Elizabeth Brookfield Holstein, b. 11 mo. 23, 1855; m. David M. Ellis, 11 mo. 11, 1882.

1617   William Hallowell Holstein, b. 8 mo. 21, 1858.
1618   Mary Alice Holstein, b. 8 mo. 21, 1865; m. William A. Arm-
        strong, Jr., 3 mo. 11, 1886.

903   Lydia Hallowell,[6] (Susanna E.,[5] Alice,[4] Zebulon,[3]
Nathan,[2] David,[1]), daughter of Joshua and Susanna E.
(Hallowell) Hallowell, was born 4 mo. 9, 1838.   She mar-
ried Clayton Yarnell.

CHILDREN OF CLAYTON AND LYDIA (HALLOWELL) YARNELL.
1619   H. Hallowell Yarnell, b. 6 mo. 18, 1862.
1620   V. Harry Yarnell, b. 6 mo. —, 1864.

904   Sarah Jane Hallowell,[6] (Susanna E.,[5] Alice,[4] Zebulon,[3] Nathan,[2] David,[1]), daughter of Joshua and Susanna
E. (Hallowell) Hallowell, was born 7 mo. 11, 1841.   She
married, first, Samuel Crook, 12 mo. 6, 1879.   She married,
second, Joseph Kelso, 12 mo. 10, 1885.

CHILD OF SAMUEL AND SARAH J. (HALLOWELL) CROOK.
1621   Alice Crook.

905   Elizabeth E. Hallowell,[6] (Susanna E.,[5] Alice,[4]
Zebulon,[3] Nathan,[2] David,[1]), daughter of Joshua and Susanna E. (Hallowell) Hallowell, was born 2 mo. 3, 1843.
She married Lukens Webster, 11 mo, 23, 1864.   He was
born 12 mo. 8, 1833.   Residence, Philadelphia, Penna.

CHILDREN OF LUKENS AND ELIZABETH (HALLOWELL) WEBSTER.
1622   Edward Burroughs Webster, b. 8 mo. 30, 1865.
1623   Clarkson Lukens Webster, b. 6 mo. 23, 1867.
1624   Edith Webster.
1625   J. Percival Webster.
1626   J. Howard Webster.

908   Ellen D. Scofield,[6] (Mary,[5] Alice,[4] Zebulon,[3] Nathan,[2] David,[1]), daughter of David and Mary (Hallowell)
Scofield, married William Coulston.   Residence, Philadel'a.

CHILDREN OF WILLIAM AND ELLEN D. (SCOFIELD) COULSTON.
1627   Lilly Malinda Coulston, m. John Armstrong.
1628   Allison H. Coulston, b. 10 mo. 12, 1876.

1629 Aramilla Coulston, deceased.
1630 Estella Coulston.   1632 David Wesley Coulston.
1631 William R. Coulston.   1633 Mary Susan Coulston.

909 Martha P. Scofield,[6] (Mary,[5] Alice,[4] Zebulon,[3] Nathan,[2] David,[1]), daughter of David and Mary (Hallowell) Scofield, was born 3 mo. 10, 1838. She married, first, Francis Bailey ; second, D. Winters ; and third, Luther Haines.

CHILDREN OF FRANCIS AND MARTHA (SCOFIELD) BAILEY.
1634 Jennie Bailey.   1635 Mary Bailey.

915 Rebecca J. Hallowell,[6] (Daniel,[5] Alice,[4] Zebulon,[3] Nathan,[2] David,[1]), daughter of Daniel and Rachel (Cook) Hallowell, was born 10 mo. 27, 1846.   She married R. H. Thomas.   Residence, Avondale, Chester County, Penna.

CHILDREN OF R. H. AND REBECCA J. (HALLOWELL) THOMAS.
1636 Elizabeth L. Thomas, b. 10 mo. 10, 1866.
1637 Rachel C. Thomas, b. 7 mo. 7, 1868.

916 Susan E. Hallowell,[6] (Daniel,[5] Alice,[4] Zebulon,[3] Nathan,[2] David,[1]), daughter of Daniel and Rachel (Cook) Hallowell, 1 mo. 24, 1850.. She married James Chambers. Residence, Avondale, Chester County, Pennsylvania.

CHILD OF JAMES AND SUSAN E. (HALLOWELL) CHAMBERS.
1638 M. Grace Chambers.

919 Hannah C. Hallowell,[6] (John,[5] Alice,[4] Zebulon,[3] Nathan,[2] David,[1]), daughter of John and Rachel C. (Carver) Hallowell, was born 7 mo. 16, 1855.   She married John Patterson.

CHILD OF JOHN AND HANNAH C. (HALLOWELL) PATTERSON.
1639 Mary Patterson.

925 Mary A. Thomas,[6] (Martha,[5] Esther,[4] Zebulon,[3] Nathan,[2] David,[1]), daughter of Marshall and Martha (Hallowell) Thomas, was born ——, and died 1876.   She married Nathan Swartley.

CHILDREN OF NATHAN AND MARY A. (THOMAS) SWARTLY.

1640 Marshall Swartley.   1641 Gertrude Swartley.

927   **Nathan H. Thomas,**[6] (Martha,[5] Esther,[4] Zebulon,[3] Nathan,[2] David,[1]), son of Marshall and Martha (Hallowell) Thomas, married Catharine Young, 1877.

CHILDREN OF NATHAN H. AND CATHARINE (YOUNG) THOMAS.

1642 Marshall Thomas,   1644 Henry Thomas.
1643 Ella Thomas.   1645 Maud Thomas.

929   **Esther H. Ramsay,**[6] (Sarah P.,[5] Esther,[4] Zebulon,[3] Nathan,[2] David,[1]), daughter of Benjamin B. and Sarah P. (Hallowell) Ramsay, married John Hampton.

CHILDREN OF JOHN AND ESTHER H. (RAMSAY) HAMPTON.

1646 Clarence Hampton.   1648 William Hampton.
1647 Howard Hampton.   1649 Bertha Hampton.

930   **Hannah W. Ramsay,**[6] (Sarah P.,[5] Esther,[4] Zebulon,[3] Nathan,[2] David,[1]), daughter of Benjamin B. and Sarah P. (Hallowell) Ramsay, married William F. Thomas.

CHILDREN OF WILLIAM F. AND HANNAH W. (RAMSAY) THOMAS.

1650 Florence Thomas.   1652 Elizabeth Thomas.
1651 Anna Thomas.

933   **Eugene S. Hallowell,**[6] (Charles,[5] Esther,[4] Zebulon,[3] Nathan,[2] David,[1]), son of Charles and Mary A. (Stewart) Hallowell, was born 1847.   He married Nellie ——.

CHILD OF EUGENE S. AND NELLIE (——) HALLOWELL.

1653 Paul Hallowell.

934   **Richard T. S. Hallowell,**[6] (Charles,[5] Esther,[4] Zebulon,[3] Nathan,[2] David,[1]) son of Charles and Mary A. (Stewart) Hallowell, married Jennie Aiken.

CHILD OF RICHARD T. S. AND JENNIE (AIKEN) HALLOWELL.

1654 Frank Hallowell.

936 Nathan M. Hallowell,[6] (Charles,[5] Esther,[4] Zebulon,[3] Nathan,[2] David,[1]), son of Charles and Mary A. (Stewart) Hallowell, married Ida Martin.

CHILD OF NATHAN M. AND IDA (MARTIN) HALLOWELL.

1655 Susan Hallowell.

939 Rev. Charles T. Hallowell,[6] (William,[5] Esther,[4] Zebulon,[3] Nathan,[2] David,[1]), son of William and Harriet W. (Thomas) Hallowell, married Rhoda Carpenter, 1873. He is a Minister of the Gospel of the Baptist Church.

CHILDREN OF CHARLES T. AND RHODA (CARPENTER) HALLOWELL.

1656 Earl Hallowell.	1658 Harriet Hallowell.
1657 Walter Hallowell.	1659 Ellenora Hallowell.

940 Horace G. J. Hallowell,[6] (William,[5] Esther,[4] Zebulon,[3] Nathan,[2] David,[1]), son of William and Matilda A. (Preston) Hallowell, married, first, Ella Miller. No issue. He married, second, Anna O'Brien.

CHILD OF HORACE G. J. AND ANNA (O'BRIEN) HALLOWELL.

1660 Morris Hallowell.

941 Hannah A. Hallowell,[6] (William,[5] Esther,[4] Zebulon,[3] Nathan,[2] David,[1]), daughter of William and Matilda A. (Preston) Hallowell, married James Yerkes, 1877.

CHILDREN OF JAMES AND HANNAH A. (HALLOWELL) YERKES.

1661 Clifford Yerkes.   1662 Anna Yerkes.   1663 Helen Yerkes.

942 Ella P. Hallowell,[6] (William,[5] Esther,[4] Zebulon,[3] Nathan,[2] David,[1]), daughter of William and Matilda A. (Preston) Hallowell, married Judson Sagebeer, 1876.

CHILDREN OF JUDSON AND ELLA P. (HALLOWELL) SAGEBEER.

1664 Maud Sagebeer.	1666 Arthur Sagebeer.
1665 Pauline Sagebeer.	

951 Israel H. Mather,[6] (Isaac,[5] Martha T.,[4] Zebulon,[3] Nathan,[2] David,[1]), son of Isaac and Ann L. (Hallowell)

74

Mather, was born May 19, 1834. He married, first, Sarah C. Lloyd, daughter of John and Sidney Lloyd, of Moreland Township, Montgomery County, Oct. 7, 1858. She died April 22, 1867. He married, second, Hannah Larzelere, daughter of Nicholas and Esther Larzelere, of Abington, October 13, 1870.

CHILDREN OF ISRAEL H. AND SARAH C. (LLOYD) MATHER.

1667   Anna L. Mather, b. May 20, 1859.
1668   Howard Mather, b. Nov. 10, 1860; m. Carrie Yerkes, (1589).

CHILDREN OF ISRAEL H. AND HANNAH (LARZELERE) MATHER.

1669   Samuel L. Mather, b. April 24, 1873; d. August 29, 1873.
1670   Esther Mather, b. Dec. 10, 1874.

954 John Mather,[6] (Edward,[5] Martha T.,[4] Zebulon,[3] Nathan,[2] David,[1]), son of Edward and Hannah P. (Paul) Mather, was born January 15, 1841. He married Tacy Williams, daughter of Charles and Alice Williams, of Whitemarsh Township, Montgomery County, March 12, 1868.

CHILDREN OF JOHN AND TACY (WILLIAMS) MATHER.

1671   Annie Mather, b. Jan. 7, 1869.
1672   Hannah Mather, b. Jan. 27, 1873.
1673   Alice Mather, b. Jan. 26, 1876.

956 Martha P. Mather,[6] (Edward,[5] Martha T.,[4] Zebuulon,[3] Nathan,[2] David,[1]), daughter of Edward and Hannah P. (Paul) Mather, was born August 12, 1844. She married Rudolph J. Mitchell, son of Pierson and Mary Ann Mitchell, of Abington, Montgomery County, April 30, 1868.

CHILD OF RUDOLPH AND MARTHA P. (MATHER) MITCHELL.

1674   Ellen Mitchell, b. May 28, 1869.

957 Philena Mather,[6] (Edward,[5] Martha T.,[4] Zebulon,[3] Nathan,[2] David,[1]), daughter of Edward and Hannah P. (Paul) Mather, was born March 30, 1848. She married Oliver Parry, son of Thomas and Lydia Parry, of Warminster Township, Bucks County, Pennsylvania, Jan. 25, 1872.

CHILDREN OF OLIVER AND PHILENA (MATHER) PARRY.

1675 Lydia C. Parry, b. January 29, 1873.
1676 Hannah M. Parry, b. June 27, 1874.
1677 Edward M. Parry, b. March 5, 1876.
1678 William C. Parry, b. August 21, 1877.

962 **Isaac Michener,**[6] (Rebecca S.,[5] Martha T.,[4] Zebulon,[3] Nathan,[2] David,[1]), son of Charles and Rebecca S. (Mather) Michener, was born July 22, 1850. He married Alice Williams, daughter of Charles and Alice Williams, of Whitemarsh Township, Montgomery County, Oct. 12, 1876.

CHILD OF ISAAC AND ALICE (WILLIAMS) MICHENER.

1679 Charles Michener, b. November 5, 1877.

975 **Thomas L. Noble,**[6] (Elizabeth H.,[5] Rebecca T.,[4] Zebulon,[3] Nathan,[2] David,[1]), son of Samuel and Elizabeth H. (Mather) Noble, was born November 24, 1857. He married ——— ———.

CHILD OF THOMAS M. AND ——— (———) NOBLE

1680 Samuel Noble.

981 **Charles Mather,**[6] (Charles,[5] Martha,[4] Zebulon,[3] Nathan,[2] David,[1]), son of Charles and Alice O. (Warner) Mather, was born April 18, 1849. He married Annie M. Bates, daughter of George and Margaret Bates, June 15, 1882. She was born April 25, 1856. Occupation, plumber. Residence, Jenkintown, Penna.

CHILDREN OF CHARLES AND ANNIE M. (BATES) MATHER.

1681 Charles Mather, b. August 19, 1883.
1682 Pierre Mather, b. January 18, 1885.
1683 Raymond Mather, b. June 28, 1886.
1684 Otis Mather, b. January 30, 1890.

986 **Martha W. Rittenhouse,**[6] (Sarah,[5] William,[4] Zebulon,[3] Nathan,[2] David,[1]), daughter of Nicholas, and Sarah (Potts) Rittenhouse, married Joseph Wise.

CHILDREN OF JOSEPH AND MARTHA W. (RITTENHOUSE) WISE.

1685 Elizabeth Wise.　　　　1686 Sarah Wise.

987 **Nicholas M. Rittenhouse,**[6] (Sarah,[5] William,[4] Zebulon,[3] Nathan,[2] David,[1]), son of Nicholas and Sarah (Potts) Rittenhouse, married Emma Omensetter.

CHILDREN OF NICHOLAS AND EMMA (OMENSETTER) RITTENHOUSE.

1687 Martin N. Rittenhouse.	1690 Anna Rittenhouse.
1688 Nicholas Rittenhouse.	1691 Carrie Rittenhouse.
1689 John Rittenhouse.	

989 **Elizabeth U. Rittenhouse,**[6] (Sarah,[5] William,[4] Zebulon,[3] Nathan,[2] David,[1]), daughter of Nicholas and Sarah (Potts) Rittenhouse, married John G. Brooke.

CHILDREN OF JOHN G. AND ELIZABETH U. (RITTENHOUSE) BROOKE·

1692 William P. Brooke.	1696 George R. Brooke.
1693 James Brooke.	1697 John M. Brooke.
1694 Mary Brooke.	1698 Anna P. Brooke.
1695 Sarah P. Brooke.	1699 Charles Brooke.

990 **Jesse Wager Walker,**[6] (Martha,[5] William,[4] Zebulon,[3] Nathan,[2] David,[1]), son of Havard and Martha (Potts) Walker, was born in Tredyffrin Township, Chester County, Pennsylvania. He received his education in the Friends' Central School and the Polytechnic School of Philadelphia. He settled in Pittsburgh, where he entered the employ of the Keystone Bridge Company. He subsequently organized the Shiffler Bridge Company and became its President. He married Isabella G. Meeker, 1872.

CHILDREN OF JESSE W. AND ISABELLA G. (MEEKER) WALKER.

1700 Anna Potts Walker.
1701 Alberta Walker, deceased. Twin with Anna P.
1702 Havard Walker, deceased.
1703 Roland Walker, deceased.

993 **William Potts Walker,**[6] (Martha,[5] William,[4] Zebulon,[3] Nathan,[2] David,[1]), son of Havard and Martha (Potts) Walker, married Fanny Baynes, daughter of Thomas and Sarah (Wetherald) Baynes. They resided at ''The Meadows,'' in Tredyffrin Township, Chester County, Pennsylvania, where he died in 1880.

CHILDREN OF WILLIAM P. AND FANNIE (BAYNES) WALKER.

1704 Miriam Kempster Walker, b. Feb. 29, 1872; d. March 30, 1889.
1705 Walter Havard Walker, b. 1878.

995 William Potts Jones,[6] (Anna,[5] William,[4] Zebulon,[3] Nathan,[2] David,[1]), son of Evan D. and Anna (Potts) Jones, was born 9 mo. 15, 1861.   He married Elizabeth C. Coulston.   Residence, Conshohocken, Pennsylvania.

CHILDREN OF WILLIAM P. AND ELIZABETH C. (COULSTON) JONES.

1706 Evan D. Jones, b. January 10, 1891.
1707 Frances C. Jones, b. September 26, 1894.

1005 Elizabeth Potts Rutter,[6] (Ellen E.,[5] Robert T.,[4] Zebulon,[3] Nathan,[2] David,[1]), daughter of Robert Lewis and Ellen Elizabeth (Potts) Rutter, was born Sept. 11, 1853. She married J. Havard Downing, son of Richard Downing of Downingtown, Pennsylvania, September 4, 1872.   Residence, near Downingtown, Pa.

CHILDREN OF J. HAVARD AND ELIZABETH P. (RUTTER) DOWNING.

1708 Richard I. Downing, b. June 21, 1873; d. April 12, 1883.
1709 Lewis Rutter Downing, b. March 19, 1875.
1710 Joseph Havard Downing, b. May 4, 1876.
1711 Ellen Potts Downing, b. August 4, 1881.

1006 Sarah Erwin Rutter,[6] (Ellen E.,[5] Robert T.,[4] Zebulon,[3] Nathan,[2] David,[1]), daughter of Robert Lewis and Ellen Elizabeth (Potts) Rutter, was born February 15, 1856. She married Joseph B. Baker, October 3, 1877.

CHILDREN OF JOSEPH B. AND SARAH E. (RUTTER) BAKER.

1712 Joseph B. Baker, b. December 20, 1882.
1713 Ellen Rutter Baker, b. December 20, 1884.

CHAPTER VII.

Seventh Generation.

1051   Eneas Franklin Smith,[7] (Sarah Ann,[6] Rachel,[5] James,[4] Samuel,[3] Daniel,[2] David,[1]), son of Robert and Sarah Ann (Hughs) Smith, married, first, Esther Smith, a second cousin, of Seville, Ohio, 1855.   After her decease he married, second, Sarah E. Moon.   When a young man he studied dentistry, but on account of ill health was compelled to relinquish the practice.   He has been engaged in farming and merchanizing.   Residence, Taloria, Lancaster County, Pennsylvania.

1052   Hannah Maria Smith,[7] (Sarah Ann,[6] Rachel,[5] James,[4] Samuel,[3] Daniel,[2] David,[1]), daughter of Robert and Sarah Ann (Hughs) Smith, was born ——, and died June 13, 1875.   She married Richard Guthrie.   Occupation, blacksmith.

CHILDREN OF RICHARD AND HANNAH MARIA (SMITH) GUTHRIE.

1714   Anna Hughs Guthrie, m. Alexander Davis.
1715   Ida Burrell Guthrie, m. Henry Ressler.
1716   Robert Smith Guthrie, m. Anna Laura Hughs, (1729).
1717   Elva Jones Guthrie, m. George Krider.
1718   John Franklin Guthrie.
1719   Walter Guthrie, d. y.
1720   George Wesley Guthrie.

1056   Samuel Wesley Smith,[7] (Sarah Ann,[6] Rachel,[5] James,[4] Samuel,[3] Daniel,[2] David,[1]), son of Robert and Sarah Ann (Hughs) Smith, married, first, Lizzie Steen, daughter of James Steen ; and second, Anna Boyer, daughter of An-

MARY MILLER-POTTS.

PAGE 547.

drew and Sarah (Pennock) Boyer.   He was a merchant at
Coatesville, for several years, and afterwards a farmer and
dealer in fine bred stock, near Cochranville, Pennsylvania.

CHILD OF SAMUEL WESLEY AND LIZZIE (STEEN) SMITH.

1721   Sarah Smith, deceased.

CHILDREN OF SAMUEL WESLEY AND ANNA (BOYER) SMITH.

1722 Robert Boyer Smith.	1724 Emma Blanche Smith.
1723 Mary Pennock Smith.	1725 Frank Wesley Smith.

1057   Capt. James Hughs,[7] (Samuel,[6] Rachel,[5] James,[4]
Samuel,[3] Daniel,[2] David,[1]), son of Samuel and Rachel (Tarrance) Hughs, was born 1832, and died March 12, 1873.
He married Mary Boyer, daughter of Andrew and Sarah
(Pennock) Boyer, 1856.   He was a farmer by occupation,
but sometimes engaged in other callings.   During the Civil
War he enlisted in the 97th Regiment, Pennsylvania Volunteers, and was commissioned Second Lieutenant of Company B.   He was mustered in August 30, 1861, and resigned
May 1, 1862, on account of broken health. · The seeds of
disease were laid during his army service, which eventually
resulted in consumption and death.   In response to the call
of the State Militia in the emergency of September, 1862,
he was commissioned and served as Captain of Company B,
2d Regiment.   Residence, Highland Township, Chester
County, Pennsylvania.

CHILDREN OF JAMES AND MARY (BOYER) HUGHS.

1726   N. C. Wilmot Hughs, m. Laura Slater.
1727   Ella Hughs, b. 18—; d. July 6, 1865.
1728   Samuel Verner Hughs, m. Mary C. McCormick.
1729   Anna Laura Hughs, m. Robert Smith Guthrie, (1716).
1730   Harry Boyer Hughs, m. Maude Gray.
1731   Walter Raleigh Hughs, m. Minnie Gray.
1732   Clara Mabel Hughs, m. Frank B. Burroughs.
1733   J. Edgar Hughs.

1058   Rachel Ann Hughs,[7] (Samuel,[6] Rachel,[5] James,[4]
Samuel,[3] Daniel,[2] David,[1]), daughter of Samuel and Rachel

(Tarrance) Hughs, married Theodore A. Baldwin, son of George Baldwin. He died September 18, 1899. Occupation, commission marketman. Residence, Parkesburg, Pa.

CHILDREN OF THEODORE A. AND RACHEL A. (HUGHS) BALDWIN.
1734   Ira H. Baldwin, m. S. Anna Wickersham.
1735   Clara E. Baldwin.
1736   Ella R. Baldwin.

1059   **Sarah Jane Hughs,**[7] (Samuel,[6] Rachel,[5] James,[4] Samuel,[3] Daniel,[2] David,[1]), daughter of Samuel and Rachel (Tarrance) Hughs, married David Watterson. She is deceased. Residence, near Parkesburg, Penna.

CHILDREN OF DAVID AND SARAH JANE (HUGHS) WATTERSON.
1737   R. Belle Watterson, m. Charles Dunn. 1895.
1738   M. Louetta Watterson, m. George Young, 1892.
1739   Frorence A. Watterson.
1740   Allie C. Watterson.
1741   Walter D. Watterson.

1061   **Joseph Hughs,**[7] (Joseph,[6] Rachel,[5] James,[4] Samnel,[3] Daniel,[2] David,[1]), son of Joseph and Sarah (Craig) Hughs, was born —— ; and died Feb. —, 1895. He married, first, Kate Swisher ; and second, Mrs. —— Hazel. He was a carpenter and contractor. Residence, Wilmington, Delaware.

CHILDREN OF JOSEPH AND KATE (SWISHER) HUGHS.
1742   Sarah Hughs, m. —— Yerger.

1062   **Henry Hughs,**[7] (Joseph,[6] Rachel,[5] James,[4] Samuel,[3] Daniel,[2] David,[1]), son of Joseph and Sarah (Craig) Hughs, married Sarah Wright. Occupation, carriage and car builder. Residence, Wilmington, Delaware.

CHILD OF HENRY AND SARAH (WRIGHT) HUGHS.
1743   Thomas M. Hughs.   1746   Georgana Hughs.
1744   Martha L. Hughs.   1747   Samuel Hughs.
1745   Elizabeth Hughs.

REV. THOMAS PLINY POTTS.

PAGE 596.

1066 **Sarah Ann Hughs,**[7] (Joseph,[6] Rachel,[5] James,[4] Samuel,[3] Daniel,[2] David,[1]), daughter of Joseph and Sarah (Craig) Hughs, married, first, Frank Hamill ; and second, Dr. John G. Gibson, a veterinary surgeon. She is a widow a second time and resides at Cochranville, Pennsylvania.

CHILD OF FRANK AND SARAH A. (HUGHS) HAMILL.

1748 Ada Hamill, m. Alexander Slack.

1069 **Mary Louisa Hughs,**[7] (Eneas,[6] Rachel,[5] James,[4] Samuel,[3] Daniel,[2] David,[1]), daughter of Eneas and Eliza (Pennock) Hughs, married Joel Harvey. Occupation, merchant. Residence, Parkesburg, Chester County, Penna.

CHILD OF JOEL AND MARY LOUISA (HUGHS) HARVEY.

1749 Eugene Harvey.

1070 **Eneas Franklin Hughs,**[7] (Eneas,[6] Rachel,[5] James,[4] Samuel,[3] Daniel,[2] David,[1]), son of Eneas and Eliza (Pennock) Hughs, married Lettie Woods, and resides in the State of Washington.

1071 **S. Emma Hughs,**[7] (Eneas,[6] Rachel,[5] James,[4] Samuel,[3] Daniel,[2] David,[1]), daughter of Eneas and Eliza (Pennock) Hughs, married Frank Tyler and lives in Illinois.

CHILD OF FRANK AND S. EMMA (HUGHS) TYLER.

1750 C. Verner Hughs.

1074 **Louisa A. Potts,**[7] (Jesse P.,[6] James W.,[5] James,[4] Samuel,[3] Daniel,[2] David,[1]), daughter of Jesse and Catharine (Mann) Potts, was born Dec. 12, 1848. She married George W. Wiandt, son of Andrew J. and Mahala Wiandt, February 27, 1871. They own and occupy a farm of 240 acres at Rippey, Greene County, Iowa.

CHILDREN OF GEORGE W. AND LOUISA A. (POTTS) WIANDT.

1751 A daughter, b. Dec. 19, 1871; d. y.

1752 Cora E. Wiandt, b. Sept. 9, 1873,

1753 Robert W. Wiandt, b. Jan. 22, 1875; d. Feb. 8, 1875.

75

1077   Franklin Pierce Potts,[7] (Jesse P.,[6] James W.,[5] James,[4] Samuel,[3] Daniel,[2] David,[1]), son of Jesse P. and Catharine (Mann) Potts, was born Nov. 13, 1853.   He married Permelia Sipe, daughter of Abraham and Charity Sipe, August 23, 1880, at Boonsboro, Iowa.   Residence, Highlands, Arapahoe County, Colorado.

CHILDREN OF FRANKLIN P. AND PERMELIA (SIPE) POTTS.

1754   Jesse Charles Potts, b. August 6, 1881.
1755   Gilford Boyce Potts, b. August 18, 1883; d. May 5, 1885.
1756   Lenora Isabella Potts, b. July 30, 1885.

1079   Joshua Potts,[7] (Jesse P.,[6] James W.,[5] James,[4] Samuel,[3] Daniel,[2] David,[1]), son of Jesse P. and Catharine (Mann) Potts, was born August 13, 1857.   He married Annie Elizabeth Law, daughter of Henry and Elizabeth Law, May 2, 1880, at Perry, Iowa.   She died December 31, 1884.   Occupation, engineer.   He spent some years in Colorado, but now resides at Perry, Dallas County, Iowa.

CHILD OF JOSHUA AND ANNIE E. (LAW) POTTS.

1757   James Potts, b. Feb. 12, 1882; d. y.
1758   Laura Louisa Potts, b. Sept. 11, 1883.

1085   William Collom,[7] (Sarah L.,[6] James W.,[5] James,[4] Samuel,[3] Daniel,[2] David,[1]), son of Jesse and Sarah Louisa (Potts) Collom, was born September 27, 1840.   He married and raised a family, but no information has been furnished. He was by occupation a farmer and resided at Mill Creek, LaPorte County, Indiana, where he was a man of considerable prominence in his community.

1094   Benjamin M. Lash,[7] (Sarah L.,[6] Ann,[5] James,[4] Samuel,[3] Daniel,[2] David,[1]), son of John and Sarah Louisa (McIntire) Lash, was born May 10, 1847.   He married Emma Herron.   Residence, Mansfield, Ohio.

CHILDREN OF BENJAMIN M. AND EMMA (HERRON) LASH.

1759   Linnie May Lash, b. July 27, 1869.
1760   John J. Lash, b. May 7, 1871.
1761   Joseph Allen Lash, b. August 28, 1873.

WILLIAM BAKER POTTS.
PAGE 509.

1096   **Alfred Lash,**[7] (Sarah L.,[6] Ann,[5] James,[4] Samuel,[3] Daniel,[2] David,[1]), son of John and Sarah Louisa (McIntire) Lash, was born Dec. 18, 1852.   He married Mary Allen. Residence, Mansfield, Ohio.

CHILD OF ALFRED AND MARY (ALLEN) LASH.

1762   Charles Lash.

1098   **Amanda McIntire,**[7] (John W.,[6] Ann,[5] James,[4] Samuel,[3] Daniel,[2] David,[1]), daughter of John Wessell and Ruth (Weigley) McIntire, was born Sept. 4, 1854.   She married William H. Wintersteen, July 24, 1878.   He is deceased.

CHILDREN OF WILLIAM AND AMANDA (MCINTIRE) WINTERSTEEN.

1763   George Wintersteen.
1764   Clara Wintersteen.
1765   Mary Wintersteen.

1100   **Samuel Weigley McIntire,**[7] (John W.,[6] Ann,[5] James,[4] Samuel,[3] Daniel,[2] David,[1]), son of John Wessell and Ruth (Weigley) McIntire, was born June 25, 1857.   He married Ellen Geary, April 1, 1881.   He is a farmer and resides near Lexington, Richland County, Ohio.

CHILD OF SAMUEL W. AND ELLEN (GEARY) MCINTIRE.

1766   Jesse McIntire.

1102   **Della McIntire,**[7] (John W.,[6] Ann,[5] James,[4] Samuel,[3] Daniel,[2] David,[1]), daughter of John Wessell and Ruth (Weigley) NcIntire, was born Dec. 8, 1859.   She married Walter Graham.

CHILD OF WALTER AND DELLA (MCINTIRE) GRAHAM.

1767   Robert Graham.

1108   **Thomas Eugene Dunshee,**[7] (Margaret, E.,[6] Ann,[5] James,[4] Samuel,[3] Daniel,[2] David,[1]), son of Thomas and Margaret E. (McIntire) Dunshee, was born August 20, 1854. He married Adella J. Cleland, daughter of Jonathan and Eliza (Barnett) Cleland, Jan. 3, 1882.   She was born April

19, 1857, and died January 24, 1897. Occupation, farmer. Residence, Lexington, Richland County, Ohio.

CHILDREN OF THOMAS EUGENE AND ADELLA J. (CLELAND) DUNSHEE.

1768 Claude C. Dunshee, b. Oct. 7, 1882.
1769 Marie Dunshee.

1110 Anna Leiby,[7] (Sarah A.,[6] Samuel,[5] James,[4] Samuel,[3] Daniel,[2] David,[1]), daughter of Jacob and Sarah Ann (Potts) Leiby, was born Oct. 19, 1843. She married Samuel Mumma, son of John and Fannie (Frantz) Mumma, Jan. 17, 1867. He was born May 21, 1821, and died July 15, 1892. Residence, Middletown, Dauphin County, Penna.

CHILDREN OF SAMUEL AND ANNA (LEIBY) MUMMA.

1770 John Mellon Mumma, b. Nov. 5, 1867.
1771 Samuel Mumma, b. Nov. 7, 1869; d. 1884.
1772 Edward Leiby Mumma, b. Jan. 13, 1871.
1773 Mabel Mumma, b. Jan. 31, 1879.

1111 Ella Leiby,[7] (Sarah A.,[6] Samuel,[5] James,[4] Samuel,[3] Daniel,[2] David,[1]), daughter of Jacob and Sarah Ann (Potts) Leiby, was born April 22, 1845. She married John W. Few, son of Kirk and Catharine (Snyder) Few, March 2, 1869. He was born Oct. 17, 1844. He has filled the positions of U. S. Railway Transfer Clerk, and Railroad Conductor on the Pennsylvania Railroad. He has served as a Member of Town Council, and is a Past Regent of the Royal Arcanum. Residence, Middletown, Dauphin County, Pennsylvania.

CHILDREN OF JOHN W. AND ELLA (LEIBY) FEW.

1774 Kirk Leiby Few, b. May 31. 1870; d. Sept. 30, 1871.
1775 John W. Few, b. July 27, 1872.
1776 Gertrude Augusta Few, b. April 25, 1875.

1112 Arabella Leiby,[7] (Sarah A.,[6] Samuel,[5] James,[4] Samuel,[3] Daniel,[2] David,[1]), daughter of Jacob and Sarah A. (Potts) Leiby, was born September 23, 1846. She married John W. Rife, son of Jacob and Mary A. (Bomberger) Rife, March 24, 1868. He was born August 14, 1856. Occupa-

MITCHEL MILLER POTTS.
PAGE 599.

SADIE GRACE BEATTY-POTTS.

PAGE 599.

tion, tanner. He served in the 194th Regiment, Penna. V. Inf., during the Civil War. He is a Republican in politics, and has filled the office of Town Council five years, and was Burgess of Middletown two terms. He was a Member of the State Legislature for 1884-5, and a Member of the 51st and 52d Congress, representing the 14th District of Pennsylvania. Residence, Middletown, Dauphin County, Pa.

CHILDREN OF JOHN W. AND ARABELLA (LEIBY) RIFE.

1777   Jacob Leiby Rife. b. Jan. 22, 1870; d. Oct. 30, 1883.
1778   William Rife, b. Dec. 27, 1873; d. May 17, 1874.

1114   Catharine Leiby,[7] (Sarah A.,[6] Samuel,[5] James, Samuel,[3] Daniel,[2] David,[1]), daughter of Jacob and Sarah A. (Potts) Leiby, was born May 12, 1850. She married Samuel Singer, son of Jacob and Mary (Laird) Singer, May 13, 1880. He was born Feb. 28, 1846, and died Oct. 16, 1889. Occupation, Tanner. He held some local offices. Residence, Middletown, Dauphin County, Pennsylvania.

CHILDREN OF SAMUEL AND CATHARINE (LEIBY) SINGER.

1779   Eva Leiby Singer, b. April 6, 1886.
1780   Samuel L. Singer, b. Nov. 6, 1887.

1116   William Leiby,[7] (Sarah A.,[6] Samuel,[5] James,[4] Samuel,[3] Daniel,[2] David,[1]), son of Jacob and Sarah Ann (Potts) Leiby, was born Jan. 9, 1856. He married Louisa D. Shurer, daughter of Frederick and Barbara (Gwinner) Shurer, February 25, 1879. She was born Nov. 9, 1860. Occupation, railroad contractor. Residence, Middletown, Dauphin County, Pennsylvania.

CHILDREN OF WILLIAM AND LOUISA D. (SHURER) LEIBY.

1781   Charles Edward Leiby, b. Oct. 30, 1880.
1782   William Jacob Leiby, b. Nov. 10, 1887.
1783   John Frederick Leiby, b. Feb. 23, 1892.
1784   Sarah Ellen Leiby, b. Sept. 5, 1893.

1120   Sarah Jane Potts,[7] (James,[6] Samuel,[5] James,[4] Samuel,[3] Daniel,[2] David,[1]), daughter of James and Mary

(Mulford) Potts, was born in Lancaster, Pennsylvania, and is the only surviving child of her parents. Through inheritance and bequest, she is possessed of a considerable estate. She has latterly resided in Philadelphia. She is an active worker in and liberal supporter of the Methodist Episcopal Church. She is a member of the Society of the Daughters of the Revolution, and is the present custodian of the sword of Major James Potts, her great grandfather. She has traveled abroad to a considerable extent.

1121   **Reuben Claude Potts,**[7] (Thomas M.,[6] Thomas J.,[5] James,[4] Samuel,[3] Daniel,[2] David,[1]), son of Thomas Maxwell and Mary (Miller) Potts, was born January 25, 1861, at the house of his grandfather Potts, in Highland Township, Chester County, Pennsylvania. He received his education in the schools of Bellville, Ohio, and Canonsburg, Pennsylvania, and learned the printing trade. He married Sarah Claribel Fife, daughter of John and Mary P. (Adams) Fife, of Canonsburg, Pa., November 30, 1882. He is a Past Grand in the Order of Old Fellows, has filled the office of School Director, is Superintendant of the Presbyterian Sunday School and an active worker in the Young Men's Christian Association. He assisted for some time in editing and publishing the *Canonsburg Herald*, but for a number of years he has been at the head of the jobbing department of the printing office of A. H. Potts & Co., at Parkesburg, Chester County, Pennsylvania.

CHILDREN OF REUBEN CLAUDE AND S. CLARIBEL (FIFE) POTTS.

1785   Ada Mary Potts, b. April 3, 1835, at Canonsburg, Penna.
1786   William Maxwell Potts, b. October 30, 1887, at Parkesburg, Pa.

1122   **Rev. Thomas Pliny Potts,**[7] (Thomas M.,[6] Thomas J.,[5] James,[4] Samuel,[3] Daniel,[2] David,[1]), son of Thomas Maxwell and Mary (Miller) Potts, was born Oct. 23, 1862, at Millville, Columbia County, Pennsylvania. He attended the schools of Canonsburg, and learned the printing trade

ADA MARY POTTS.

R. CLAUDE POTTS.   S. CLARIBEL POTTS.

WILLIAM MAXWELL POTTS.

PAGE 598.

in his father's office.   He studied medicine and attended
lectures at Baltimore in 1884-5, but having decided to enter
the ministry, did not finish the full course.   He was a teacher
for.some time, entered Washington and Jefferson College and
graduated in the Class of 1891 with the degree of A. B.
He studied theology in the Western Theological Seminary
and graduated in the Class of 1894.   He accepted a call to
the pastorate of the Presbyterian Churches of Vanport, In-
dustry and Bethlehem, in the Presbytery of Allegheny, Pa.
He was ordained at the Vanport Church on July 3, 1894.
Residence, Vanport, Beaver County, Pennsylvania.

1123   **William Baker Potts,**[7] (Thomas M.,[6] Thomas J.,[5]
James,[4] Samuel,[8] Daniel,[2] David,[1]), son of Thomas Maxwell
and Mary (Miller) Potts, was born March 6, 1865, at Millville, Columbia County, Pa.   He received his education in
the schools of Canonsburg, and learned the printing trade
in his father's office.   He also worked in printing offices at
Parkesburg and at Pittsburgh.   In 1891 he became a member of the firm of Potts Brothers, grocers and dealers in
China-ware, at Canonsburg, Pennsylvania.

1124   **Mitchel Miller Potts,**[7] (Thomas M.,[6] Thomas J.,[5]
James,[4] Samuel,[3] Daniel,[2] David,[1]), son of Thomas Maxwell
and Mary (Miller) Potts, was born January 5, 1867, at Bellville, Richland County, Ohio.   He received his education
in the schools of Canonsburg, and learned the printing trade
in his father's office.   He engaged in the retail grocery business and was a member of the firm of Hill & Potts, which
was succeeded by the firm of Potts Brothers, of which he is
a member, dealers in groceries and China-ware.   He married Sadie Grace Beatty, of Akron, Ohio, and daughter of
Jonathan (deceased) and Emeline (Hookey) Beatty, Sept.
26, 1900.   The ceremony was performed by Rev. Thomas
Pliny Potts, at Vanport, Penna.   Residence, Canonsburg,
Washington County, Pennsylvania.

1125 Louis Maxwell Potts, Ph. D,[7] (Thomas M.,[6] Thomas J.,[5] James,[4] Samuel,[3] Daniel,[2] David,[1]), son of Thomas Maxwell and Mary (Miller) Potts, was born October 30, 1876, at Canonsburg, Pennsylvania. He graduated from the Canonsburg High School in 1891, and from Washington and Jefferson College in 1896 with the degree of A. B. He taught in the Washington (Pa.) High School in 1896-7, after which he entered Johns Hopkins University at Baltimore, and received the degree of Doctor of Philosophy in June 1900. At Washington and Jefferson College he was awarded the Samuel Jones Prize of $100, and at Johns Hopkins University he was selected as one of the Student Assistant Teachers during the last year of his course. At this writing he is employed as an assistant in the laboratory of the Rowland Multiplex Telegraph Company, with headquarters at Baltimore, Maryland.

1126 Anna Eudora Margaret Potts,[7]). James Carter,[6] Thomas J.,[5] James,[4] Samuel,[3] Daniel,[2] David,[1]), daughter of James Carter and Grizelle (McIntire) Potts, was born September 17, 1861. She is a member of the Society of the Daughters of the Revolution, and an active worker in the Presbyterian Church. She married Robert Castner. He is an attorney-at-law, and a member of the Cleveland bar. Residence, Cleveland, Ohio.

1128 Harry Lee Potts,[7] (James C.,[6] Thomas J.,[5] James,[4] Samuel,[3] Daniel,[2] David,[1]), son of James Carter and Grizelle (McIntire) Potts, was born April 5, 1866. He is a druggist and resides at Bellville, Richland County, Ohio. He married Eudora Hamilton, daughter of John Addison and Elmira (Garber) Hamilton, December 27, 1892, at Bellville. She was born October 8, 1869.

CHILDREN OF HARRY LEE AND EUDORA (HAMILTON) POTTS.

1787 Eva Elmira Potts, b. September 12, 1895.
1788 Mary Gazelle Potts, b. June 12, 1898.

LOUIS MAXWELL POTTS, PH. D.

PAGE 600.

1129 Linnie May Potts,[7] (James Carter,[6] Thomas J.,[5] James,[4] Samuel,[3] Daniel,[2] David,[1]), daughter of James Carter and Grizelle (McIntire) Potts, was born April 5, 1866. She is a twin with Harry Lee Potts. She married Dr. Marion E. Blair, April 11, 1888. Mrs. Blair and her daughter reside at Bellville, Richland County, Ohio.

CHILD OF DR. MARION E. AND LINNIE MAY (POTTS) BLAIR.

1789 Gladys Gazelle Blair, b. Nov. 14, 1889

1187 Asahel Walker Cook,[7] (Elizabeth,[6] Mary,[5] Elizabeth,[4] Peter,[3] Elizabeth,[2] David,[1]), daughter of George W. and Elizabeth (Walker) Cook, was born October 26, 1832. He married Hannah C. Garretson, daughter of Daniel and Anne (Cook) Garretson. She was born Dec. 17, 1833.

CHILDREN OF ASAHEL W. AND HANNAH C. (GARRETSON) COOK.

1790 Theresa Cook, b. Aug. 12, 1855.
1791 Anne F. Cook, b. June 24, 1857; d. May 18. 1895; m —— Jones.
1792 George W. Cook, b. Oct. 10, 1859.
1793 Sarah Jane Cook, b. Dec. 31, 1861; d. y.
1794 Mary Ellen Cook, b. Dec. 31, 1861.
1795 Ida J. Cook, b. Dec, 27, 1864; m. ———— Hileman.
1796 Melissa G. Cook, b. Dec. 13, 1866.

1230 Lewis M. Cleaver,[7] (Amos G.,[6] John,[5] John,[4] Peter,[3] Elizabeth,[2] David,[1]), son of Amos G. and Amelia (Morris) Cleaver, was born Nov. 14, 1837. He is a merchant and prominent citizen of East Bethlehem, Washington County, Penna. He married Mary M. Kenny, Dec. 6, 1873. No issue.

1231 Annie C. Cleaver,[7] (Amos G.,[6] John,[5] John,[4] Peter,[3] Elizabeth,[2] David,[1]), daughter of Amos G. and Amelia (Morris) Cleaver, was born May 20, 1841. She married Ahira Jones, Dec. 25, 1860. He was born April 30, 1840, in Maine. Residence, East Bethlehem, Penna.

CHILDREN OF AHIRA AND ANNIE C. (CLEAVER) JONES.

1797 Millie S. Jones, b. July 21, 1862; m. James T. Espy.

76

1798 Fannie A. Jones, b. March 6, 1864; m. Richard Watkins.
1799 Rollin R. Jones, b. March 27, 1866; m. Mary Miller.
1800 Ida R. Jones, b. May 11, 1863; d. April 20, 1897.
1801 Edwin G. Jones, b. July 16, 1870; m. Agnes Malone.
1802 Oliver H. Jones, b. April 18, 1873; m. Maggie Jones.
1803 Carrie Jones, b. August 20, 1875.

1232. Hiram T. Cleaver,[7] (Amos G.,[6] John,[5] John,[4] Peter,[3] Elizabeth,[2] David,[1]), son of Amos G. and Amelia (Morris) Cleaver, was born Nov. 20, 1843. He married Margaret Woodfield, Dec 25, 1867.

CHILDREN OF HIRAM T. AND MARGARET (WOODFIELD) CLEAVER.

1804 Ira A. Cleaver, b. April 19, 1869; m. May Williams.
1805 Mahlon L. Cleaver, b. Jan. 19, 1871; m. Bertha Seybert.
1806 Ella Cleaver, b. April 6, 1874; m. Frank Reynolds, 1897.
1807 Clara A. Cleaver, b. April 9, 1876.

1233 William H. Cleaver,[7] (Amos G.,[6] John,[5] John,[4] Peter,[3] Elizabeth,[2] David,[1]), son of Amos G. and Amelia (Morris) Cleaver, was born Feb. 3, 1846. He married Annie E. White, Nov. 27, 1870. She died January 3, 1889. Residence, East Bethlehem, Washington, County, Penna.

CHILDREN OF WILLIAM H. AND ANNIE E. (WHITE) CLEAVER.

1808 Nellie J. Cleaver, b. Sept. 23, 1872.
1809 Lenora J. Cleaver, b. August 1, 1876; m. James Hill.
1810 Mary A. Cleaver, b. June 24, 1879.

1234 Elizabeth H. Cleaver,[7] (Amos G.,[6] John,[5] John,[4] Peter,[3] Elizabeth,[2] David,[1]), daughter of Amos G. and Amelia (Morris) Cleaver, was born June 17, 1848. She married Mahlon Linton, Dec. 26, 1867.

CHILDREN OF MAHLON AND ELIZABETH (CLEAVER) LINTON.

1811 Lawrence Linton, b. April 12, 1872.
1812 Gertrude Linton, b. July 6, 1877.
1813 Naomi Linton, b. February 7, 1880.
1814 Edith Linton, b. May 9, 1887.

1235 Samuel M. Cleaver,[7] (Amos G.,[6] John,[5] John,[4] Peter,[3] Elizabeth,[2] David,[1]), son of Amos G. and Amelia

(Morris) Cleaver, was born April 18, 1851. He married, first, Ella Curry, September 26, 1876. She died June 3, 1896. He married second, Mina K. Farquhar June 23, 1897.

CHILD OF SAMUEL M. AND ELLA (CURRY) CLEAVER.

1815 Frank W. Cleaver, b. Aug. 13, 1878; m. Florence Wickerham.

1236 John W. Cleaver,[7] (Amos G.,[6] John,[5] John,[4] Peter,[3] Elizabeth,[2] David,[1]), son of Amos G. and Amelia (Morris) Cleaver, was born Sept. 27, 1863. He married Ida J. Drake, Dec. 15, 1886.

CHILDREN OF JOHN W. AND IDA J. (DRAKE) Cleaver.

1816 Hattie Cleaver, b. November 22, 1787.
1817 Amelia Cleaver, b. December 21, 1889.
1818 Harry Cleaver, b. June 29, 1893.
1819 Cora Cleaver, b. October 2, 1898.

1291 Harry Altemus,[7] (William,[6] Jane,[5] Anna,[4] Stephen,[3] Nathan,[2] David,[1]), son of William and Sarah (Johnson) Altemus, married Mary O'Neil.

CHILDREN OF HARRY AND MARY (O'NEIL) ALTEMUS.

1820 Sarah Altemus.	1822 Anna Altemus.
1821 Thomas Altemus.	1823 Hannah Altemus.

1298 Emma Altemus,[7] (Thomas N.,[6] Jane,[5] Anna,[4] Stephen,[3] Nathan,[2] David,[1]), daughter of Thomas and Sarah (Murray) Altemus, married Irwin Zimmerman.

CHILDREN OF IRWIN AND EMMA (ALTEMUS) ZIMMERMAN.

1824 Helen Zimmerman.

1300 Emma O'Neil,[7] (Morris,[6] Esther,[5] Anna,[4] Stephen,[3] Nathan,[2] David,[1]), daughter of Morris and Caroline (Milton) O'Neill, married Cornelius H. Linton.

CHILDREN OF CORNELIUS AND EMMA (O'NEIL) LINTON.

1825 Edwin Linton.	1826 Elizabeth M. Linton.

1301 Sarah O'Neil,[7] (Morris,[6] Esther,[5] Anna,[4] Stephen,[3]

Nathan,[2] David,[1]), daughter of Morris and Caroline (Milton) O'Neil, married William W. Cotter.

CHILDREN OF WILLIAM W. AND SARAH (O'NEIL) COTTER.

1827   Ethel N. Cotter.   1828   Maurice Cotter.

1359 John F. Griggs,[7] (T. Virginius,[6] Abigail,[5] Nathan,[4] Stephen,[3] Nathan,[2] David,[1]), son of T. Virginius and Melinda A. (Mann) Griggs, was born 4 mo. 21, 1859. He married Etta Neff, 1 mo. 1, 1883.

CHILDREN OF JOHN F. AND ETTA (NEFF) GRIGGS.

1829   Russell Griggs, b. 4 mo. 24, 1884.
1830   Ray Griggs, b. 4 mo. 23, 1885; d. 12 mo. 14, 1885.

1367   Ellis Potts Miller,[7] (Margaret,[6] Joseph,[5] Nathan,[4] Stephen,[3] Nathan,[2] David,[1]), son of David R. and Margaret (Potts) Miller, was born 5 mo. 7, 1860, and died 3 mo. 31, 1887, at Harrisburg, Penna., aged 26 years, 10 months, 24 days. He was a very intelligent, genial and conscientious gentleman. When a lad he served as a page in the Legislature. For several years he had charge of a department in a large notion store in Philadelphia, but on account of ill health he was compelled to resign his position. Subsequently he and his brothers began preparations to engage in mercantile business at Harrisburg, but his early death put an end to these plans. He was greatly interested in family history and had collected much data concerning the descendants of Nathan Potts, (11), which has been incorporated into this work.

1368   Herman Potts Miller,[7] (Margaret,[6] Joseph,[5] Nathan,[4] Stephen,[3] Nathan,[2] David,[1]), son of David R. and Margaret (Potts) Miller, was born 12 mo. 15, 1863, in Fairview Township, York County, Pennsylvania. He has long filled official positions at the Capitol at Harrisburg. He began, in January 1876 as a page in the Senate, and has risen step by step to the position which he now holds, that

ELLIS POTTS MILLER.
PAGE 604.

of Senate Librarian, having been appointed to that office on July 1, 1890. His long service is an evidence of intelligence, capability and integrity. Since 1887 he has annually assisted in the compiling of the State Manual, " *Smull's Legislative Hand Book.*" As a member and trustee of the Board of Trade, he takes an active interest in the welfare of his adopted city. He married Martha P. Jones, (997), daughter of Evan D. and Anna T. (Potts) Jones, of Conshohocken, Penna., August 12, 1891. Residence, Harrisburg, Pennsylvania.

CHILDREN OF HERMAN P. AND MARTHA P. (JONES) MILLER.

1831　Anna Margaret Miller, b. June 20, 1892.
1832　Herman Potts Miller, Jr., b. August 10, 1895.
1833　Evan Jones Miller, b. Jan. 6, 1897.
1834　Lillian Jones Miller, b. Jan. 6, 1897.

1369 William Potts Miller,[7] (Margaret,[6] Joseph,[5] Nathan,[4] Stephen,[3] Nathan,[2] David,[1]), son of David R. and Margaret (Potts) Miller, was born 12 mo. 22, 1865, in Yocumtown, York County, Pennsylvania. Since 1887 he has been an assistant in the Senate Library at Harrisburg. He resides at Harrisburg, Penna.

1370 Albert O. Potts,[7] (George,[6] Joseph,[5] Nathan,[4] Stephen,[3] Nathan,[2] David,[1]), son of George and Barbara Ann (Ort) Potts, was born 10 mo. 6, 1860. He married Lyda Blane.

CHILDREN OF ALBERT O. AND LYDA (BLANE) POTTS.

1835　George Potts.

1388 Hanson S. Riegel,[7] (Ann,[6] George,[5] Nathan,[4] Stephen,[3] Nathan,[2] David,[1]), son of Henry and Ann (Potts) Riegel was born 11 mo. 7, 1856. He married Alwilda Fry, 9 mo. 30, 1880. Occupation engineer. Residence, Harrisburg, Pennsylvania.

1836   Ross Milton Riegel, b. 10 mo. 31, 1881.
1837   DeWitt Riegel, b. 3 mo. 30, 1884.

1390   Alice M. Riegel,[7] (Ann,[6] George,[5] Nathan,[4] Stephen,[3] Nathan,[2] David,[1]), daughter of Henry and Ann (Potts) Riegel, was born 11 mo. —, 1861.   She married Abner Forrest 12 mo. 24, 1880.   Residence, Harrisburg.

CHILDREN OF ABNER AND ALICE M. (RIEGEL) FORREST.
1838   Charles Forrest.   1839   Harry Allen Forrest.

1394   Mary E. Wells,[7] (Elmira J.,[6] George,[5] Nathan,[4] Stephen,[3] Nathan,[2] David,[1]), daughter of Joseph and Elmira J. (Potts) Wells, married Jacob Sourbeer.

CHILDREN OF JACOB AND MARY E. (WELLS) SOURBEER.
1840   Amy Almira Sourbeer, b. 5 m. 6, 1881.
1841   James H. Sourbeer, b. 6 mo. 11, 1883.

1419   Bartlet Crone,[7] (Ann,[6] Jane,[5] Nathan,[4] Stephen,[3] Nathan,[2] David,[1]), son of Elijah and Ann (Powell) Crone, married Sarah Boring.

CHILD OF BARTLET AND SARAH (BORING) CRONE.
1842   Harry Crone.

1420   Andrew Crone,[7] (Ann,[6] Jane,[5] Nathan,[4] Stephen,[3] Nathan,[2] David,[1]), son of Elijah and Ann (Powell) Crone, married Mary Ortmyer.

CHILD OF ANDREW AND MARY (ORTMYER) CRONE.
1843   Ira Crone.

1426   Alice M. Griest,[7] (Harriet,[6] Jane,[5] Nathan,[4] Stephen,[3] Nathan,[2] David,[1]), daughter of Jonathan and Harriet (Powell) Griest, was born 3 mo. 14, 1858.   She married Robert Stonecipher.

CHILDREN OF ROBERT AND ALICE M. (GRIEST) STONECIPHER.
1844   Bennie M. Stonecipher.   1845.   Anna Jane Stonecipher.

1461 Louis M. Childs,[7] (Jacob,[6] Ann T.,[5] Mary,[4] Alice,[3] Nathan,[2] David,[1]), son of Jacob and Lydia (Foss) Childs, was born August 19, 1852. He married Alice G. Hibberd, daughter of Norris and Eliza (Moore) Hibberd, September 26, 1889. She was born March 26, 1864. He is an attorney at law and is a member of the Montgomery County Bar, residing at Norristown, Pennsylvania.

CHILDREN OF LOUIS M. AND ALICE G. (HIBBERD) CHILDS.

1846 Alice H. Childs, b. February 10, 1891.
1847 Marjorie Childs, b. September 25, 1893.
1848 Louis M. Childs, b. June 2, 1900.

1466 Martha Kane,[7] (Abram,[6] Elizabeth,[5] Mary,[4] Alice,[3] Nathan,[2] David,[1]), daughter of Abram and Charlotte (McVaughn) Kane, married Charles Spencer.

CHILDREN OF CHARLES AND MARTHA (KANE) SPENCER.

1849 Sallie Spencer.   1850 Abram L. Spencer.

1471 Margaret Elizabeth Peterman,[7] (Issacher,[6] Jacob,[5] Priscilla,[4] Alice,[3] Nathan,[2] David,[1]), daughter of Issacher and Miriam (Fox) Peterman, married William E. Crissey.

CHILD OF WILLIAM E. AND MARGARET E. (PETERMAN) CRISSEY.

1851 Frank Crissey.

1472 Jacob Peterman,[7] (Issacher,[6] Jacob,[5] Priscilla,[4] Alice,[3] Nathan,[2] David,[1]), son of Issacher and Miriam (Fox) Peterman, married Elizabeth Zellner.

CHILDREN OF JACOB AND ELIZABETH (ZELLNER) PETERMAN.

1852 Jacob Peterman.   1855 Mary Peterman.
1853 Issacher Peterman.   1856 Anna H. Peterman.
1854 Thomas P. Peterman.

1473 Emma S. Peterman,[7] (Issacher,[6] Jacob,[5] Priscilla,[4] Alice,[3] Nathan,[2] David,[1]), daughter of Issacher and Miriam (Fox) Peterman, married Thomas Pilson.

CHILDREN OF THOMAS AND EMMA S. (PETERMAN) PILSON.
1857   Miriam Pilson.   1858   Nellie Pilson.

1474   Ellen P. Peterman,[7] (Issacher,[6] Jacob,[5] Priscilla,[4] Alice,[3] Nathan,[2] David,[1]), daughter of Issacher and Miriam (Fox) Peterman, married John Little.

CHILDREN OF JOHN AND ELLEN P. (PETERMAN) LITTLE.
1859   Mabel Little.   1860   Edna Little.

1476   Miriam K. Peterman,[7] (Issacher,[6] Jacob,[5] Priscilla,[4] Alice,[3] Nathan,[2] David,[1]), daughter of Issacher and Miriam (Fox) Peterman, married Charles Clark.

CHILDREN OF CHARLES AND MIRIAM K. (PETERMAN) CLARK.
1861   Helen Clark.   1862   Mildred Clark.

1479   Clara Peterman,[7] (John E.,[6] Jacob,[5] Priscilla,[4] Alice,[3] Nathan,[2] David,[1]), daughter of John E. and Mary (West) Peterman, married William Chester.

CHILD OF WILLIAM AND CLARA (PETERMAN) CHESTER.
1863   Clarance Chester.

1482   Horace B. Vaughn,[7] (Matilda M.,[6] Ann,[5] Priscilla,[4] Alice,[3] Nathan,[2] David,[1]), son of Jacob and Matilda M. (Ramsay) Vaughn, married Mary ———.

CHILD OF HORACE B. AND MARY (———) VAUGHN.
1864   Matilda M. Vaughn.

1485   Anna Vaughn,[7] (Matilda M.,[6] Ann,[5] Priscilla,[4] Alice,[3] Nathan,[2] David,[1]), daughter of Jacob and Matilda M. (Ramsay) Vaughn, married John Hines.

CHILD OF JOHN AND ANNA (VAUGHN) HINES.
1865   George Hines.

1486   Caroline Vaughn,[7] (Matilda M.,[6] Ann,[5] Priscilla,[4] Alice,[3] Nathan,[2] David,[1]), daughter of Jacob and Matilda

M. (Ramsay) Vaughn, married Samuel Dyer. Residence, Chester, Delaware County, Pennsylvania.

CHILDREN OF SAMUEL AND CAROLINE (VAUGHN) DYER.
1866 Anna Dyer. 1867 Helen Dyer. 1868 John Dyer.

1489 Louisa Weik,[7] (Maria,[6] Ann,[5] Priscilla,[4] Alice,[3] Nathan,[2] David,[1]), daughter of John and Maria (Ramsay) Weik, married Dr. William Bell.

CHILD OF DR. WILLIAM AND LOUISA (WEIK) BELL.
1869 John Bell.

1492 Henry H. Brognard,[7] (Caroline,[6] Ann,[5] Priscilla,[4] Alice,[3] Nathan,[2] David,[1]), son of L. N. and Caroline (Ramsay) Brognard, married Mary ———.

CHILDREN OF HENRY AND MARY (———) BROGNARD.
1870 Mary Brognard. 1871 Anna Brognard.

1501 Kate Harris,[7] (Maria,[6] Benjamin F.,[5] Priscilla,[4] Alice,[3] Nathan,[2] David,[1]), daughter of John and Maria (Peterman) Harris, married ——— Wentz.

CHILD OF ——— AND KATE (HARRIS) WENTZ.
1872 Thomas Wentz.

1527 Anna Maria Everman,[7] (George W.,[6] Alice,[5] Priscilla,[4] Alice,[3] Nathan,[2] David,[1]), daughter of George W. and Edith T. (Bennett) Everman, George Reeves.

CHILDREN OF GEORGE AND ANNA MARIA (EVERMAN) REEVES.
1873 Everman Reeves. 1875 Edith Reeves.
1874 George Reeves.

1528 Alice P. Everman,[7] (George W.,[6] Alice,[5] Priscilla,[4] Alice,[3] Nathan,[2] David,[1]), daughter of George W. and Edith T. (Bennett) Everman, married ——— Clinton.

CHILD OF ——— AND ALICE P. (EVERMAN) CLINTON.
1876 Edith B. Clinton.

77

1530 Sarah B. Everman,[7] (George W.,[6] Alice,[5] Priscilla,[4] Alice,[3] Nathan,[2] David,[1]), daughter of George W. and Edith T. (Bennett) Everman, married Isaac Elliott.

CHILDREN OF ISAAC AND SARAH B. (EVERMAN) ELLIOTT.

1877 Edith Elliott.
1878 Arnold Elliott.
1879 Hannah Elliott.
1880 Lenora Elliott.

1533 Edith B. Petty,[7] (Anna Maria,[6] Alice,[5] Priscilla,[4] Alice,[3] Nathan,[3] David,[1]), daughter of Thomas Robert and Anna Maria (Everman) Petty, married Salm Hudson.

CHILD OF SALM AND EDITH B. (PETTY) HUDSON.

1881 Mabel Hudson.

1542 Harry Hallowell,[7] (Benjamin,[6] Job,[5] Hannah,[4] Alice,[3] Nathan,[2] David,[1]), son of Benjamin and Rebecca (Whitney) Hallowell, married Mary ————.

CHILD OF HARRY AND MARY (————) HALLOWELL.

1882 Benjamin Hallowell.

1543 Emily T. Otto,[7] (Rebecca M.,[6] Mary R.,[5] Hannah,[4] Alice,[3] Nathan,[2] David,[1]), daughter of John B. and Rebecca M. (Tyson) Otto, married Fred W. Swartz.

CHILDREN OF FRED W. AND EMILY T. (OTTO) SWARTZ.

1883 Charles S. Swartz.
1884 Amy W. Swartz.
1885 Fannie E. Swartz.

1544 Ella W. Otto,[7] (Rebecca M.,[6] Mary R.,[5] Hannah,[4] Alice,[3] Nathan,[2] David,[1]), daughter of John B. and Rebecca M. (Tyson) Otto, married Lewis P. Lauger.

CHILDREN OF LEWIS P. AND ELLA W. (OTTO) LAUGER.

1886 Rebecca Lauger.
1887 Edgar Lauger.
1888 Elva Lauger.

1545 Harry R. Otto,[7] (Rebecca M.,[6] Mary R.,[5] Hannah,[4] Alice,[3] Nathan,[2] David,[1]), son of John B. and Rebecca M. (Tyson) Otto, married Jennie Garwood.

CHILDREN OF HARRY R. AND JENNIE (GARWOOD) OTTO.

1889 Larua Mary Otto.   1891   Charles A. Otto.
1890 Nettie A. Otto.

1557 Zebulon Smith,[7] (Thomas,[6] Zebulon,[5] Martha,[4] Alice,[3] Nathan,[2] David,[1]), son of Thomas and Hannah (—— ——) Smith, married ——— ————.

CHILDREN OF ZEBULON AND ——— (———) SMITH.

1892 Nellie Smith.

1589 Carrie T. Yerkes,[7] (Martha,[6] William,[5] Ann,[4] Zebulon,[3] Nathan,[2] David,[1]), daughter of William and Martha (Thomas) Yerkes, was born June 27, 1861.   She married Howard Mather, (1668), December 19, 1883.

CHILDREN OF HOWARD AND CARRIE T. (YERKES) MATHER.

1893 Sarah C. Mather, b. October 21, 1884.
1894 Frank Howard Mather, b. December 3, 1885.
1895 Emily T. Mather, b. August 12, 1890

1627 Lilly Malinda Coulston,[7] (Ellen D.,[6] Mary,[5] Alice,[4] Zebulon,[3] Nathan,[2] David,[1]), daughter of William and Ellen D. (Scofield) Coulston, married John Armstrong.

CHILDREN OF JOHN AND LILLY M. (COULSTON) ARMSTRONG.

1896 Estella Armstrong.
1897 Ellen Mary Armstrong.

CHAPTER VIII.

Eighth Generation.

1716 **Robert Smith Guthrie,**[8] (Hannah M.,[7] Sarah A.,[6] Rachel,[5] James,[4] Samuel,[3] Daniel,[2] David,[1]), son of Richard and Hannah Maria (Smith) Guthrie, married Anna Laura Hughs, (1729), daughter of Capt. James and Mary (Boyer) Hughs. He is a farmer, and resides near Cochranville, Chester County, Pennsylvania.

CHILD OF R. SMITH AND ANNA L. (HUGHS) GUTHRIE.
1898 Mabel Guthrie.

1734 **Ira H. Baldwin,**[8] (Rachel A.,[7] Samuel,[6] Rachel,[5] James[4] Samuel,[3] Daniel,[2] David,[1]), son of Theodore and Rachel Ann (Hughs) Baldwin, married S. Anna Wickersham, daughter of John Wickersham, November 29, 1900. He is merchant at Parkesburg, Chester County, Pennsylvania.

1748 **Ada Hamill,**[8] (Sarah A.,[7] Joseph,[6] Rachel,[5] James,[4] Samuel,[3] Daniel,[2] David,[1]), daughter of Frank and Sarah A, (Hughs) Hamill, married Alexander Slack. She resides at Cochranville, Chester County, Pennsylvania.

CHILD OF ALEXANDER AND ADA (HAMILL) SLACK.
1899 Pauline Slack.

1797 **Millie S. Jones,**[8] (Annie C.,[6] Amos G.,[6] John,[5] John,[4] Peter,[3] Elizabeth,[2] David,[1]), daughter of Ahira and Annie C. (Cleaver) Jones, was born July 21, 1862. She married James T. Espy, son of James and Susan, (Sill) Espy, September 14, 1884. Occupation, plumber. Residence, Canonsburg, Washington County, Pennsylvania.

CHILDREN OF JAMES T. AND MILLIE S. (JONES) ESPY.

1900 James Cleaver Espy, b. July 30, 1883.
1901 Walter R. Cleaver, b. May 20, 1885; d. July 28, 1895.

1798 Fannie A. Jones,[8] (Annie C.,[7] Amos G.,[6] John,[5] John,[4] Peter,[3] Elizabeth,[2] David,[1]), daughter of Ahira and Annie C. (Cleaver) Jones, was born March 6, 1864. She married Richard Watkins, October 28, 1884.

CHILD OF RICHARD AND FANNIE A. (JONES) WATKINS.

1902 Fred A. Watkins, b. August 3, 1883.

1799 Rollin R. Jones,[8] (Annie C.,[7] Amos G.,[6] John,[5] John,[4] Peter,[3] Elizabeth,[2] David,[1]), son of Ahira and Annie B, (Cleaver) Jones, was born March 28, 1866. He married Mary Miller, February 24, 1897.

CHILD OF ROLLIN R. AND MARY (MILLER) JONES.

1903 Harry M. Jones, b. December 18, 1898.

1801 Edwin G. Jones,[8] (Annie C.,[7] Amos G.,[6] John,[5] John,[4] Peter,[3] Elizabeth,[2] David,[1]), son of Ahira and Annie C. (Cleaver) Jones, was born July 16, 1870. He married Agnes Malone, daughter of George T. and Jemima (Wilson) Malone, July 13, 1893. Residence, Urichsville, Ohio.

CHILD OF EDWIN G. AND AGNES (MALONE) JONES.

1904 Annie Mae Jones, b. May 29, 1894.

1802 Oliver H. Jones,[8] (Annie C.,[7] Amos G.,[6] John,[5] John,[4] Peter,[3] Elizabeth,[2] David,[1]), son of Ahira and Annie C. (Cleaver) Jones, was born April 18, 1873. He married Maggie Jones February 8, 1894.

CHILD OF OLIVER H. AND MAGGIE (JONES) JONES.

1905 Dulcie Jones, b. March 23, 1895; d. May 20, 1897.

Tabulated Pedigree.

Charts Showing Descendants of David Potts.

The tabulated pedigree given on the following pages is a recapitulation of the foregoing records, showing six generations of descendants of David Potts in the male line. For want of space descendants in female lines are not carried down in these tables. The numbers in the last column of the first chart, correspond to the individual numbers in the foregoing text, and also to the numbers used in the succeeding tables, where later generations appear. The surname *Potts* is omitted where the name of wife or husband is given.

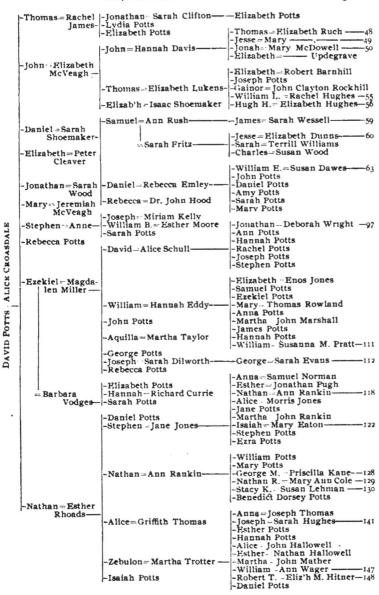

DAVID POTTS . ALICE CROASDALE

```
-Thomas=Rachel   |-Jonathan· Sarah Clifton----Elizabeth Potts
      James-     |-Lydia Potts
                 |-Elizabeth Potts              -Thomas =Elizabeth Ruch ----48
                    |-Johan=Mary ----,----49
                 |-Johan=Hannah Davis----       -Jonah· Mary McDowell----50
                                                 -Elizabeth=---- Updegrave
-John· Elizabeth
     McVeagh —                                  -Elizabeth=Robert Barnhill
                                                -Joseph Potts
                 -Thomas-:Elizabeth Lukens-     -Gainor=John Clayton Rockhill
                                                -William L. =Rachel Hughes —55
                 |-Elizab'h = Isaac Shoemaker   |-Hugh H. - Elizabeth Hughes—56

                 |-Samuel=Ann Rush----          -James- Sarah Wessell----59
-Daniel =Sarah
     Shoemaker-
                       =Sarah Fritz----         -Jesse=Elizabeth Dunns----60
-Elizabeth=Peter                                -Sarah=Terrill Williams
     Cleaver                                    -Charles=Susan Wood

                                                -William E. =Susan Dawes—63
-Jonathan=Sarah  -Daniel=Rebecca Emley--        -John Potts
     Wood                                       -Daniel Potts
-Mary=Jeremiah   -Rebecca=Dr. John Hood         -Amy Potts
     McVeagh                                    -Sarah Potts
                 -Joseph= Miriam Kelly          -Mary Potts
-Stephen--Anne—  -William B.=Esther Moore       -Jonathan--Deborah Wright —97
-Rebecca Potts   -Sarah Potts                   -Ann Potts
                                                -Hannah Potts
                 -David=Alice Schull            -Rachel Potts
                                                -Joseph Potts
                                                -Stephen Potts

                                                -Elizabeth· Enos Jones
-Ezekiel=Magda-                                 -Samuel Potts
     len Miller —                               -Ezekiel Potts
                 -William=Hannah Eddy----       -Mary-- Thomas Rowland
                                                -Anna Potts
                 -John Potts                    -Martha  John Marshall
                                                -James Potts
                 -Aquilla=Martha Taylor         -Hannah Potts
                                                -William- Susanna M. Pratt—111
                 -George Potts
                 -Joseph· Sarah Dilworth----    -George=Sarah Evans ----112
                 -Rebecca Potts
                                                -Anna=Samuel Norman
                 -Elizabeth Potts               -Esther=Jonathan Pugh
    =Barbara      -Hannah--Richard Currie        -Nathan=Ann Rankin----118
     Vodges—      -Sarah Potts                   -Alice · Morris Jones
                                                -Jane Potts
                 -Daniel Potts                  -Martha  John Rankin
                 -Stephen -Jane Jones----       -Isaiah=Mary Eaton----122
                                                -Stephen Potts
                                                -Ezra Potts

                                                -William Potts
                                                -Mary Potts
                 -Nathan=Ann Rankin----         -George M. ·Priscilla Kane--128
                                                -Nathan R. =Mary Ann Cole —129
                                                -Stacy K.· Susan Lehman —130
-Nathan=Esther                                  -Benedict Dorsey Potts
     Rhoads—
                                                -Anna=Joseph Thomas
                 -Alice=Griffith Thomas         -Joseph =Sarah Hughes----141
                                                -Esther Potts
                                                -Hannah Potts
                                                -Alice · John Hallowell ·
                                                -Esther- Nathan Hallowell
                 -Zebulon=Martha Trotter —      -Martha - John Mather
                                                -William -Ann Wager ----147
                 -Isaiah Potts                  -Robert T. -Eliz'h M. Hitner—148
                                                -Daniel Potts
```

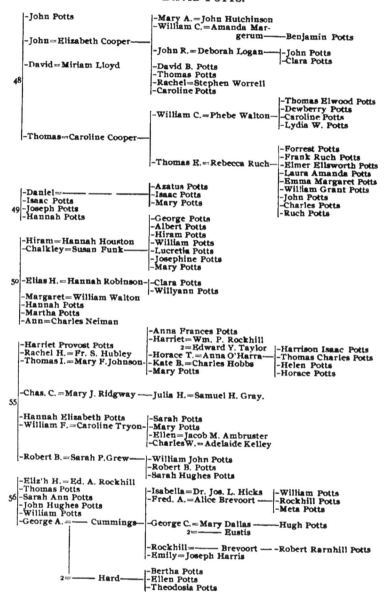

-John Potts

-John=Elizabeth Cooper——

48

-David=Miriam Lloyd

-Mary A.=John Hutchinson
-William C.=Amanda Mar-
             gerum——Benjamin Potts
-John R.=Deborah Logan——-John Potts
                               -Clara Potts
-David B. Potts
-Thomas Potts
-Rachel=Stephen Worrell
-Caroline Potts

-Thomas=Caroline Cooper——

-William C.=Phebe Walton——
-Thomas Elwood Potts
-Dewberry Potts
-Caroline Potts
-Lydia W. Potts

-Thomas E.=Rebecca Ruch——
-Forrest Potts
-Frank Ruch Potts
-Elmer Ellsworth Potts
-Laura Amanda Potts
-Emma Margaret Potts
-William Grant Potts
-John Potts
-Charles Potts
-Ruch Potts

49
-Daniel=————————
-Isaac Potts
-Joseph Potts
-Hannah Potts

-Azatus Potts
-Isaac Potts
-Mary Potts

-Hiram=Hannah Houston
-Chalkley=Susan Funk——
-George Potts
-Albert Potts
-Hiram Potts
-William Potts
-Lucretia Potts
-Josephine Potts
-Mary Potts

50
-Elias H.=Hannah Robinson-
-Clara Potts
-Willyann Potts

-Margaret=William Walton
-Hannah Potts
-Martha Potts
-Ann=Charles Neiman

-Harriet Provost Potts
-Rachel H.=Fr. S. Hubley
-Thomas I.=Mary F. Johnson-
-Anna Frances Potts
-Harriet=Wm. P. Rockhill
     2=Edward Y. Taylor
-Horace T.=Anna O'Harra——
-Kate B.=Charles Hobbs
-Mary Potts

-Harrison Isaac Potts
-Thomas Charles Potts
-Helen Potts
-Horace Potts

55
-Chas. C.=Mary J. Ridgway——Julia H.=Samuel H. Gray.

-Hannah Elizabeth Potts
-William F.=Caroline Tryon-
-Sarah Potts
-Mary Potts
-Ellen=Jacob M. Ambruster
-Charles W.=Adelaide Kelley

-Robert B.=Sarah P. Grew——
-William John Potts
-Robert B. Potts
-Sarah Hughes Potts

-Eliz'h H.=Ed. A. Rockhill
-Thomas Potts
56-Sarah Ann Potts
-John Hughes Potts
-William Potts
-George A.=——— Cummings-
-Isabella=Dr. Jos. L. Hicks
-Fred. A.=Alice Brevoort ——
-William Potts
-Rockhill Potts
-Meta Potts

-George C.=Mary Dallas ———Hugh Potts
     2=——— Eustis

-Rockhill=——— Brevoort ——-Robert Rarnhill Potts
-Emily=Joseph Harris

2=——— Hard——
-Bertha Potts
-Ellen Potts
-Theodosia Potts

```
-Rachel=Eneas Hughs          -Jesse P.=Catharine Mann —-Neye Potts
-Triplet sons                -Thomas Stroud Potts        -Louisa A.=G. W. Wiandt
-Hannah Potts                -Charlotte=John Scott        -Brady Potts
-James W.=Margaret Stroud-   -Sarah L.=Jesse Collom       -Stephen Decatur Potts
-Ann=Thomas McIntire         -Margaret=William Baker      -Frank. P.=Permelia Sipe
                             -Rachel Potts                -Willey Potts
-Eliza Potts                 -Rebecca Potts               -Joshua=Annie E. Law
                             -Phebe=Jesse Collom
                                                          -Andrew R. Potts
59 -Samuel=Margaret Sheafer-  -Sarah A.=Jacob Leiby       -James Bernard Potts
                             -James=Mary Mulford          -James Potts
   -Hannah=Isaac Tarrance                                 -Sarah Jane Potts

   -Sarah=Joseph Tarrance                                 -R.Claude=S.ClaribelFife
                                                          -Rev. Thomas Pliny Potts
                             -Th. Maxwell=Mary Miller-    -William Baker Potts
   -Thomas J.=MargaretCarter-                             -Mitchel Miller Potts
                                                          -Louis Maxwell Potts

                                                          -Anna E. M.=R. Castner
                             -James C.=Grizelle McIntire- -Mary Louisa Potts
                                                          -HarryL.=Dora Hamilton
                             -Sarah Elizabeth Potts       -Linnie M.=Dr.M.E.Blair

   -Sarah=Vincent Benham     -William=Anna Wilson—————    -Mary Etta Potts
                                                          -Thomas Wilson Potts

   -Nancy=Robert Hewson      -Joseph T.=M.Eliz'h Hamill-  -Nellie Louisa Potts
                                                          -Joseph Edgar Potts
                                                          -Charles Edwin Potts
   -Jane=William Lawrence    -Mary Anna Potts             -Mary Bertha Potts
60                                                        -Anna Marguerite Potts
   -Samuel Potts             -Alfred H.=Alice Young————   -Alfred Hamilton Potts
                                                          -Margaret Reinee Potts
                                                          -Philip Clive Potts
                                                          -Rachel Inez Potts
   -John D.=Rebecca Shaw———— -Mary Elizabeth Potts        -Stella Henrietta Potts
                                                          -Zella Marietta Potts
   -Jesse C.=Eunice U. Walker- -Sarah Benham Potts        -Thomas Alva Potts
                             -Jesse Walker Potts          -James Alpha Potts

                                                          -John Wesley Potts
                                                          -James B. Potts
                                                          -Mary Jane Potts
                             -William=Malinda Spindler-   -Charles Potts
                             -Catharine=Benj. J. Davis    -Lenna Potts
                                                          -George Allen Potts
                                                          -William Frederick Potts

   -Charles D.=M. A. Opdyke— -Benj. J.=Mary Meredith ——— -Laura Augusta Potts
                                                          -Clifton Meredith Potts

                             -Joseph=Isabel Ralston————   -Charles Bartley Potts
                             -John Potts                  -Minnie Potts
                                                          -Carrie Potts

                             -Daniel W.=Arilla Lewis ———  -Nellie Potts
                             -Susan=Lyttle Moore          -Lewis Potts
                             -Margaret Potts              -Sarah Potts
   -Lucinda Potts            -Mary D.=Morgan Howard       -Jennie Potts
63
                             -Susan=George S. Cole
                             -Christiana=Ph. Bosenbury
                             -Mary=Horace P. Quick
   -Joseph=CatharineManning- -Jane=Henry P. VanFleet
                             -Martha=John Hoffman
                             -Lewis Cass Potts
                             -Elma E. Potts
                             -Frances A.=Peter B. Hall

                             -Amy Potts
                             -Catharine=John Park
                             -Levi Potts
   -Daniel E.=A.Rockafellow— -John=Jane Cook ————————— -George W. Potts
                             -Sarah Potts
___
78      2=Eliz'h Wagoner—    -Sarah Potts
                             -Elizabeth Potts
                             -Susan Potts
```

```
                                        -Eliza Potts              -Charles W. Potts
      -Joseph.- ---- ---- ----          -Maria Potts             -Edwin S. Potts
                                        -John Potts               -George C. Potts
                                                                  -John Potts
 '97|                                   -William Potts            -James Potts
      -John W. - Elizabeth Coyle----    -Joseph B. = Emily Bush   -Ella C. = Geo. W. Thorpe
      -Elizabeth - George Fore                                    -Elizabeth F. Potts
      -Sarah = Joseph Strain            -A. Wilson Potts
      -Mary - John Belch                                          -Frank M. Potts
      -Alice = Jonah Blackburn          -James M. = Mary F.Malven- -Mary Potts
                                                                  -John Charles Potts
                                        -John C. Potts
                                                                  -Effie M. Potts
                                        -George T. - Ann E. Peck --Clara Potts
      -Martha M. - Owen M. Evans        -Susan E. = John Chapman  -Samuel W. Potts
          2 = ---- Yeager                                         -Nannie E. Potts
          3 - Thomas Harvey
                                        -Susan M. = John S. Kennedy
                                        -Thomas E. - Mat Johnson ---Frank Keith Potts
      -Thos. P. = Isabella Reinhardt    -Walter Raleigh Potts
          2 - Abbie M. Butcher-         -Nathan Reinhardt Potts
  111|                                  -Lydia S.  Davis J. Webster
                                        -Annie I.  Jon'h'n J. Webster
                                        -Isaac Reinhardt Webster


      -Ezekiel = Joanna Sheldrake -     -William H. Potts
      -Hannah Potts                     -Susan Massey Potts
                                        -George M. Potts
                                        -William N. Potts
      -Joseph Potts                     -Ida M. = John J. Gehret
      -Joel Potts
      -William Potts                    -Harriet Potts            -Albert O. - Lyda Blane
      -Mary - George Wells              -Margaret - David R. Miller -J. Clayton Potts
  112|-Joshua Potts                     -George = Barbara A. Ort --- -Emma J. Potts
      -Hannah Potts                     -Ann Potts                -Anna E. Potts
      -Randal Potts
      -Dilworth Potts                                             -William Potts
                                        -Andrew B. = Susan Roop-- -Andrew Potts
                                                                  -Maud Potts
      -Harriet - John Wambaugh
      -John Potts                       -William C. - Martha Thomas- -Ross R. Potts
      -Abigail - James Griggs               2 = Susan Kline       -Florence R. Potts
      -Joseph - Eliza Blymyer----
      -Stephen Potts                                              -Berva = John G. Way
                                        -Joseph R. - Malinda Ross-- -Alletta M. Potts
                                                                  -Minnie E. Potts
      -William = Lanah Kunkle----       -Eliza Jane Potts
                                        -Rankin C. Potts
  118|                                  -Lucinda = William Barton
                                        -Annie - Martin Laird
                                        -William K. = Anna Getz
                                        -Sarah Etta Potts
                                        -Joseph Elmer Potts
                                        -Penrose L. = Ann Huey---- --Marlin J. Potts
                                        -Emerson H. Potts
                                        -Harriet Cecelia Potts

      -George - Mary Watts ----
      -Jane - Jacob Powell             -Ann - Henry Reigel
      -Anna Potts                       -Harriet = Thomas Grier---- -Bessie H. Potts
      -Rankin Potts                     -Elmira J. - Joseph Wells  -Clista H. Potts
      -Isaiah Potts                     -Susanna - Wm. Mackibben
                                        -Andrew W. - Jane Ely----  -M. Abbie Potts
                                        -Eliza = David Black       -Emma Potts
      -Kezia = ---- Trimble             -Jane Potts
      -Jane = ---- Polley               -Milton G. = Ella Ringler---- -George C. Potts
  122|-Martha Potts                                               -Emily Elizabeth Potts
      -Mary Ann Potts                                             -Ellen Alwilda Potts
      -William Potts
```

```
|-Ferdinand = Sarah Saylor————————Harriet = Samuel Markey
|-Henrietta = ———— Ransom
|-Benedict D. = Elizabeth M. ——
128|-Clementine Potts
|-Elenora Potts
|-Mary Ann Potts
                                            |-Juliet C. Potts
|-Chas. T. = Henrietta M. Badger—|
                                            |-Virginia Potts
                                            |-Charles Theodore Potts
|-Percival M. = Eliza'h Chapline —|-Percival Potts
                                            |-Nina = ———— Tilden
                                            |-William Potts

                                            |-Caroline L. = T. J. Wentworth
            2 = Louisa Cauffman —|-Howard Cameron Potts
129|-Cornelia Potts                          |-Edith C. Edwin Meredith
|-Elenora = Augustus B. Shipley            |-Charlotte Potts
|-Howard N. = Mary A. Sommer               |-Clara Potts
|-Alfred Bonsal Potts
|-Caroline Augusta Potts
|-Caroline A. = Charles G. Sower
|-Anna Shipley Potts
|-Reginald Heber = ——— ——— ——— —Nathan R. Potts
|-Anna K. = William S. Whitney
|-Imogene B. = Ambrose E. Witmer|-Dr. Charles Sower Potts
|-Francis C. = Emma Bigler————|-William A. Potts
                                            |-Leonora Potts
|-Serena M. Potts                           |-Emma F. Potts
130|-Emily Potts
|-Priscilla = Charles Sheafer

|-Hannah = William Stroud
141|-Martha = ———— Thornton              |-Hannah Potts
|-Samuel = Jane Young————            |-Elwood Potts
                                            |-Samuel Potts

|-Zebulon Potts
|-J. Wager Potts
|-Sarah Nicholas Rittenhouse
147|-Martha = Havard Walker
|-Tabitha Potts
|-Anna T. = Evan D. Jones
|-Tabitha F. = Geo. R. Rittenhouse

|-Henry Clay Potts
|-Ellen E. Robert L. Rutter
|-E. Channing = Caroline E. Cox—|-Caroline D. Potts
                                            |-Robert Potts
148|-Martha T. = Dr. Chas. Sheafer
                                            |-Brita H. John D. Paist
                                            |-Helen R. Potts
|-William W. = Ella Holstein————|-Carrie Potts
                                            |-Abbie Holstein Potts
                                            |-Ella Holstein Potts
```

Supplement.

[MEMORANDUM. The following records, furnished by William Theodore Gauss, of Colorado Springs, Colorado, came to hand after the printing of the book was nearly completed, and too late to be incorporated in consecutive order.—T. M. P.]

Third Generation.

38 **Elizabeth Potts,**[3] (Ezekiel,[2] David,[1]), daughter of Ezekiel and Barbara (*Vodges*) Potts, was born 9 mo., 14, 1753, and died about 1820. She married Andrew Kennedy, under a Pennsylvania license dated February 17, 1774. Andrew Kennedy was born in Ireland, about 1751. He enlisted, March 3, 1777, at Philadelphia, in the Fourth Pennsylvania Regiment, Continental Line, in the Revolutionary War. The Regiment was commanded by Col. Lambert Cadwallader, and participated in the battles of Brandywine, Germantown, Jamestown, Yorktown, and was at Valley Forge. He was honorably discharged in 1781.

About 1794, a committee of the Friends Yearly Meeting purchased a part of the Langhorne Estate, in Bucks County, including the mansion house and about 400 acres of land, with the intention of establishing a Friends School there. But afterward not liking it so well, it was sold in the Philadelphia Exchange to Andrew Kennedy, who purchased it at a very low price.* Kennedy made some repairs to the mansion house before the close of the century. Andrew Kennedy died Sep. 23, 1811. The wills of both Andrew and Elizabeth are registered at Philadelphia. Andrew is described as manufacturer of Philadelphia, and Elizabeth as widow of Northern Liberties.

CHILDREN OF ANDREW AND ELIZABETH (POTTS) KENNEDY.

1906 Andrew Kennedy. Died while a Cadet at West Point.
1907 George Washington Kennedy. Was living in 1818.
1908 Robert Kennedy, m. Ann Pennington.
1909 Mary Kennedy, m. Peter Tilly, April 23, 1795. Son, John.
1910 Elizabeth Kennedy, b. 1779; d. 1850; m. Col. Kennedy Long.
1911 Susan Kennedy, m. Dr. Michael Leib.
1912 Eleanor Kennedy, m. John Paul Schott, Jr., May 9, 1810.

* See Pennsylvania Magazine of History and Biography, Vol. VII, page 81.

Fourth Generation.

1908   Robert Kennedy,[4] (Elizabeth,[3] Ezekiel,[2] David,[1]), son of Andrew and Elizabeth (Potts) Kennedy, was a keeper of Naval stores at Philadelphia. He is said to have been married twice. The records of the Second Presbyterian Church of Philadelphia, give the marriage of Robert Kennedy and Ann Pennington, as having been consumated on February 1, 1810, but it does not appear whether she was the mother of his children or not.

CHILDREN OF ROBERT AND ——— (———) KENNEDY.

1913	Andrew Kennedy.	1917	Anna Kennedy.
1914	Charles Kennedy.	1918	Louisiana Kennedy.
1915	John Kennedy.	1919	Aurelia Kennedy.
1916	Robert Kennedy.		

1910   Elizabeth Kennedy,[4] (Elizabeth,[3] Ezekiel,[2] David,[1]), daughter of Andrew and Elizabeth (Potts) Kennedy, was born in 1779, at or near Germantown, Pennsylvania. She married Col. Kennedy Long, November 16, 1797, as it appears by the records of the Second Presbyterian Church, of Philadelphia. Col. Long commanded the 27th Maryland Regiment in the War of 1812. Brig. Gen. Striker reports the 27th Regiment under Col. Long, as "having in a particular manner distinguished itself in the defense of Baltimore. It was unsurpassed for bravery, resolution and enthusiasm." He was born in 1763 in Ireland, and died February 27, 1821, in Baltimore, Maryland. Elizabeth died in 1850, at Pittsfield, Illinois.

CHILDREN OF COL. KENNEDY AND ELIZABETH (KENNEDY) LONG.

1920   Eliza Long, b. Aug. 12, 1802; d. Nov. 25, 1870; m. Dr. George Balfour.
1921   Andrew Kennedy Long, b. June 29, 1804; d. October 6, 1866; m. Marian Lowry Donaldson.
1922   George Long, died in youth.
1923   Mary Jane Long, b. 1807; d. ——; m. Dr. Moses L. Knapp.
1924   Thomas Jefferson Long, b. June 25, 1808; m. Eliza'h M. Irwin.
1925   James Hutton Long, b. August 28, 1809; m. Eliza Jane Noyes.
1926   William Henry Long, b. ——; d. ——.
1927   Emelia Juliana Long, b. January 19, 1819; d. February 9, 1881; m. Dr. Thomas Worthington.

1911 Susan Kennedy,[4] (Elizabeth,[3] Ezekiel,[2] David,[1]), daughter of Andrew and Elizabeth (Potts) Kennedy, married Dr. Michael Leib, of Philadelphia. Dr. Leib was a powerful factor in Pennsylvania politics for many years. He was elected a Member of Congress in 1802, and to a second term in 1804. He was elected a Member of Assembly in 1807, and United States Senator in 1809. In 1814, he was made Postmaster of Philadelphia, but the opposition was so strong against the appointment, that he was afterward removed, and soon dropped out of politics.

CHILDREN OF DR. MICHAEL AND SUSAN (KENNEDY) LEIB.

1928 Dr. George Leib.　　　　1930 Elizabeth Leib.
1929 Dr. Henry Leib.　　　　 1931 Lavinia Leib.

Fifth Generation.

1920 Eliza Long,[5] (Elizabeth,[4] Elizabeth,[3] Ezekiel,[2] David,[1]), daughter of Col. Kennedy and Elizabeth (Kennedy) Long, was born August 12, 1802, in Baltimore, Maryland; and died November 25, 1870, at Pittsfield, Illinois. She married Dr. George Balfour, of Norfolk, Virginia. He was a Surgeon in the U. S. Navy.

CHILD OF DR. GEORGE AND ELIZA (LONG) BALFOUR.

1932 Elena M. Balfour, died in infancy.

1921 Capt. Andrew Kennedy Long,[5] (Elizabeth,[4] Elizabeth,[3] Ezekiel,[2] David,[1]), son of Col. Kennedy and Elizabeth (Kennedy) Long, was born June 29, 1804, in Baltimore; and died October 6, 1866. He was a Captain in the U. S. Navy. He married Marian Lowry Donaldson, daughter of James Lowry Donaldson, of Baltimore, (who was killed at the battle of North Point in the defense of Baltimore in the War of 1812), April 18, 1837. She was born March 21, 1813; and died January 11, 1870.

CHLIDREN OF ANDREW K. AND MARIAN L. (DONALDSON) LONG.

1933 James Donaldson Long, b. Jan. 11, 1838; d. 1885, Santos, Brazil.
1934 Marian Elizabeth Long, b. Jan. 8, 1841; m. Thomas B. Rodgers.

1935   Andrew Kennedy Long, b. April 6, 1843; d. 1871; m. Elizabeth Donnell Foster.
1936   George Worthington Long, b. May 17, 1846; d. April 7, 1892.
1937   William St. Clair Long, b. Dec. 28, 1850; d. 1893.
1938   Edgar St. John Long, b. May 6, 1855; d. Jan. 10, 1870.

1923   Mary Jane Long,[5] (Elizabeth,[4] Elizabeth,[3] Ezekiel,[2] David,[1]), daughter of Col. Kennedy and Elizabeth (Kennedy) Long, born 1807, in Baltimore, and died at Terre Haute, Indiana, married Dr. Moses L. Knapp.

CHILDREN OF DR. MOSES L. AND MARY JANE (LONG) KNAPP.

1939   Virginia Knapp, m. Aug. Nippert.
1940   Laura Knapp.
1941   Helen Knapp, m. —— Hageman.
1942   Julia Knapp, m. Dr. —— Chandler.
1943   Mary Jane Knapp.
1944   Moses Knapp, d. unm.

1924   Thomas Jefferson Long,[5] (Elizabeth,[4] Elizabeth,[3] Ezekiel,[2] David,[1]), son of Col. Kennedy and Elizabeth (Kennedy) Long, was born June 25, 1808, in Baltimore, Maryland ; and died at Barry, Illinois. He married Elizabeth M. Irwin, June 12, 1834. She was born October 9, 1815 ; and died March 1, 1887, at Louisiana, Missouri.

CHILDREN OF THOMAS J. AND ELIZABETH M. (IRWIN) LONG.

1945   Adelaide Jane Long, m. Vincent Ridgeley.
1946   Margaret E. Long, d. unm.
1947   Josephine E. Long, d. unm.
1948   Mary Alice Long, m. John H. Gamble.
1949   William Henry Long, m. Jane Hendricks.
1950   Thomas Catesby Long, m. Julia Klein.
1951   Isidore Eliza Long, m. George Harvey.
1952   Zillah Vincent Long, m. George Blair.
1953   Marian Emily Long, m. John Travis Orr.

1925   James Hutton Long,[5] (Elizabeth,[4] Elizabeth,[3] Ezekiel,[2] David,[1]), son of Col. Kennedy and Elizabeth (Kennedy) Long, was born August 28, 1809, in Baltimore, Md. He married Eliza Jane Noyes, November 16, 1848. She was born April 27, 1819.

CHILDREN OF JAMES HUTTON AND ELIZA JANE (NOYES) LONG.

1954 Michael Kennedy Long, b. August 18, 1849.
1955 Elena Balfour Long, b. May 5, 1851; d. January 11, 1891.
1956 Minna Louisa Long, b. Sept. 9, 1853; m. Henry Abbott, June
       1877. Children, 1 Mary Elitha, 2 Helen Kennedy, 3 Emily
       Rae, 4 Merton Henry, 5 James Hubert, 6 Minna May Mason.
1957 William Talcott Long, b. Oct. 6, 1855; m. Nancy Olive Orr, Sep.
       8, 1886.. Children, 1 Alan, 2 Frederick William, 3 Helen
       Elitha, 4 James Henry.
1958 Elitha Jane Long, b. March 14, 1858; m. Loraine A. Chamber-
       lain, June 18, 1893. He was born Nov. 18, 1856.

1927   **Emelia Juliana Long,**[5] (Elizabeth,[4] Elizabeth,[3]
Ezekiel,[2] David,[1]), daughter of Col. Kennedy and Elizabeth
(Kennedy) Long, was born January 19, 1819, in Baltimore ;
and died February 9, 1881, at Pittsfield, Illinois. She married Dr. Thomas Worthington, January 19, 1837, at Spring-
field, Illinois. He was born June 11, 1808, in Anderson
County, Tennessee ; and died November 14, 1888, at Pittsfield, Illinois.

CHILDREN OF DR. THOMAS AND EMELIA J. (LONG) WORTHINGTON.

1959 William Baker Worthington, d. y.
1960 Emily Worthington, b. November 19, 1839.
1961 James Kennedy Worthington, b. Sep. 1, 1842; d. Aug. 12, 1889;
       m. Harriet Elizabeth Sneed.
1962 Elizabeth Worthington, b. May 28, 1844; d. February 19, 1873;
       m. Alexander Mirrielees.
1963 George Balfour Worthington, b. Jan. 15, 1846; d. Apr. 5, 1895;
       m. Hannah M. Criswell.
1964 Mary Katharine Worthington, b. March 5, 1848; m. Dr. John
       W. Graham, June 25, 1884.
1965 Thomas Worthington, b. June 8, 1850; m. Miriam Weeks Mor-
       rison.
1966 John Grimshaw Worthington, b. Dec. 26, 1852; m. Jessamine
       Matthews.
1967 Helen Worthington, b. Jan. 29, 1855; m. William T. Gauss.
1968 Jesse Worthington, d. y.
1969 Andrew Kennedy Worthington, b. Aug. 25, 1859. Physician.
       Residence, Denver, Colorado.

Sixth Generation.

1934   **Marian Elizabeth Long,**[6] (Andrew Kennedy,[5]
Elizabeth,[4] Elizabeth,[3] Ezekiel,[2] David,[1]), daughter of Andrew K. and Marian L. (Donaldson) Long, was born Janu-

ary 8, 1841, in Logan County, Illinois.   She married Col. Thomas Blackwood Rodgers, October 24, 1865, at St. Johns Episcopal Church, Carlisle, Pennsylvania.   Residence, St. Louis, Missouri.

CHILDREN OF COL. THOMAS B. AND MARIAN E. (LONG) RODGERS.

1970   James Lowry Donaldson Rodgers, b. Nov. 1, 1868.
1971   James Russell Rodgers, b. Jan. 12, 1871.
1972   Thomas Blackwood Rodgers, b. March 12, 1877.
1973   Andrew Kennedy Rodgers, b. July 7, 1881.

1935   Andrew Kennedy Long,[6] (Andrew K.,[5] Elizabeth,[4] Elizabeth,[3] Ezekiel,[2] David,[1]), son of Andrew K. and Marian L. (Donaldson) Long, was born April 6, 1843.   He was a Colonel in the U. S. Army, and died at Washington, D. C., 1871.   He married Elizabeth Donnell Foster.

CHILDREN OF ANDREW K. AND ELIZABETH D. (FOSTER) LONG.

1974   Mary Foster Long, b. August 23, 1868.
1975   Emily Foster Long, b. June 10, 1871.
1976   Elizabeth Donnell Long, b. March 11, 1873.
1977   Henry Donnell Foster Long, b. Sept. 20, 1874.

1961   James Kennedy Worthington,[6] (Emelia Juliana,[5] Elizabeth,[4] Elizabeth,[3] Ezekiel,[2] David,[1]), son of Doctor Thomas and Emelia J. (Long) Worthington, was born Sep. 1, 1842, at Pittsfield, Illinois; and died August 12, 1889, at Kirkwood, Mo.   He married Harriet Elizabeth Sneed.

CHILDREN OF JAMES K. AND HARRIET E. (SNEED) WORTHINGTON.

1978   James Alexander Worthington, b. April 5, 1872; m. Grace Mae Slinkard, May 1, 1901.
1979   Samuel Sneed Worthington, d. unm.
1980   Arthur Thomas Worthington, b. Nov. 10, 1875.
1981   Anna Emily Worthington, d. unm.
1982   Jesse Kennedy Worthington, b. October 27, 1880.
1983   Harriet Elizabeth Worthington, b. February 25, 1884.
1984   Frank Worthington, died in infancy.

1962   Elizabeth Worthington,[6] (Emelia J.,[5] Elizabeth,[4] Elizabeth,[3] Ezekiel,[2] David,[1]), daughter of Dr. Thomas and Emelia J. (Long) Worthington, was born May 28, 1844, at

Pittsfield, Illinois ; and died February 19, 1873, at the same place.   She married Alexander Mirrielees, Dec. 2, 1869.

CHILD OF ALEX. AND ELIZABETH (WORTHINGTON) MIRRIELEES.

1985   Margaret Ronald Mirrielees, b. Sept. 30, 1871; m. Lydell Baker.

1963   **George Balfour Worthington,**[6] (Emelia Juliana,[5] Elizabeth,[4] Elizabeth,[3] Ezekiel,[2] David,[1]), son of Dr. Thomas and Emelia J. (Long) Worthington, was born Jan. 15, 1846, at Pittsfield, Illinois ; and died April 5, 1895, at Barry, Ill. He married Hannah M. Criswell, October 19, 1867.

CHILDREN OF GEORGE B. AND HANNAH (CRISWELL) WORTHINGTON

1986   Paul Worthington, b. July 19, 1868.
1987   Minna Worthington, b. August 28, 1870; m. Albyn L. Adams.
1988   Helen Worthington, b. Jan. 21, 1873; m. Maj. Purinton, 1899.
1989   George Worthington, d. y.
1990   Robert Kennedy Worthington, b. 1876.

1964   **Mary Katharine Worthington,**[6] (Emelia Juliana,[5] Elizabeth,[4] Elizabeth,[3] Ezekiel,[2] David,[1]), daughter of Dr. Thomas and Emelia J. (Long) Worthington, was born March 5, 1848, at Pittsfield, Illinois.   She married Dr. John W. Graham, son of Andrew and Jane White (Brown) Graham, June 25, 1884, at Pittsfield, Ills.   He was born May 24, 1843, in Westmoreland County, Pennsylvania.   Residence, 1007 Pennsylvania Avenue, Denver, Colorado.

1965   **Thomas Worthington,**[6] (Emelia J.,[5] Elizabeth,[4] Elizabeth,[3] Ezekiel,[2] David,[1]), son of Dr. Thomas and Emelia J. (Long) Worthington, was born June 8, 1850, in Tenn. He married Miriam Weeks Morrison, November 16, 1892.

CHILD OF THOMAS AND MIRIAM W. (MORRISON) WORTHINGTON.

1991   Isaac L. Morrison Worthington, b. Sept. 12, 1893.

1966   **John Grimshaw Worthington,**[6] (Emelia Juliana,[5] Elizabeth,[4] Elizabeth,[3] Ezekiel,[2] David,[1]), son of Dr. Thomas and Emelia J. (Long) Worthington, was born Dec, 26, 1852.   He married Jessamine Matthews, March 29, 1881.

CHILD OF JOHN G. AND JESSAMINE (MATTHEWS) WORTHINGTON.

1992 Julian Matthews Worthington, b. July 19, 1884.

1967 Helen Worthington,[6] (Emelia J.,[5] Elizabeth,[4] Elizabeth,[3] Ezekiel,[2] David,[1]), daughter of Dr. Thomas and Emelia Juliana (Long) Worthington, was born Jan. 29, 1855, at Pittsfield, Illinois.   She married William Theodore Gauss, son of Charles W. Gauss, and grandson of Carl Friedrich Gauss, the mathematician and scientist, June 24, 1875.   He was born July 1, 1851, in Chariton County, Missouri.   Residence, Colorado Springs, Col.   Children born at St. Louis.

CHILDREN OF WILLIAM T. AND HELEN (WORTHINGTON) GAUSS.

1993 Carl Friedrich Gauss, b. October 19, 1878.
1994 Helen Worthington Gauss, b. April 9, 1881.
1995 (Wm.) Theodore Worthington Gauss, b. September 4, 1884.
1996 Helen W. Gauss, b. July 18, 1887; d. Feb. 8, 1889.

Seventh Generation.

1985 Margaret Ronald Mirrielees,[7] (Elizabeth,[6] Emelia J.,[5] Elizabeth,[4] Elizabeth,[3] Ezekiel,[2] David,[1]), daughter of Alexander and Elizabeth (Worthington) Mirrielees, was born Sept. 30, 1871, at Pittsfield, Ills.   She married Lydell Baker, Sept. 30, 1897.   Residence, Portland, Oregon.

1987 Minna Worthington,[7] (George B.,[6] Emelia J.,[5] Elizabeth,[4] Elizabeth,[3] Ezekiel,[2] David,[1]), daughter of Geo. Balfour and Hannah (Criswell) Worthington, was born Aug. 28, 1870, at Pittsfield, Illinois.   She married Dr. Albyn Lincoln Adams, son of James Wilberforce and Lee (Bowman) Adams, of Jacksonville, Illinois, June 11, 1896.   Residence, Jacksonville, Illinois, where all the children were born.

CHILDREN OF DR. ALBYN L. AND MINNA (WORTHINGTON) ADAMS.

1997 Albyn Worthington Adams, b. March 5, 1897.
1998 Helen Wilcox Adams, b. September 2, 1899.
1999 Mary Catharine Graham Adams, b. Oct. 7, 1900; d. July 23, 1901.

· PART IV.
Corrections and Additions.

PART IV.

CORRECTIONS AND ADDITIONS.

The following pages contain information received after the foregoing pages were printed, the correction of such errors as have been noticed, and supplemental matter of more or less interest.

PART I.

Page 48.   29th line from top, for "son" read "daughter"

Page 76.   14th line from top, for "azure two bars" read "azure two bars or"

Page 77.   Two black marbles in the chancel of the church at Great Ellingham are thus inscribed :

Jacet PHILLIPUS POTTS, hoc sub Marmore
Domini ROGERI Baronetti e Filijs,
Amice Lector, parce (sis) Lachrymis tuis,
Morique discas. quem legis, Quondam fuit,
Rarum beatae Exemplar Innocentiae,
Virtute Amicus, et (quod Instar omnium)
Pietate clarus, in Parentes et Deum,
Sed in Juventa louguidus Morbo gravi,
Valedixit Orbi huic lubrico, et plenus Fide
Tenace, laetus suaviterque obdormijit,
Anno Aetatis 27,
1698.

MEMENTO-MORI.
Here lyeth the Body of Elizabeth, the Wife of Charles Potts, Citizen,

and Merchant Tayler of London, who departed this Life the 2d of Sept.
Ao. Dni. 1706, at Kensington, in Com. Midd: aged 21 Years.

> Not Youth, nor Beauty, Wealth, Descent or Lands,
> Can charm pale Death, or stay his cruel hands.

Page 85.   5th line from top.   John Potts, son of Ralph, was baptized in 1544, and Nicholas in 1546.

Page 95.   The following is an English translation of the biographical sketch, in Dutch, commencing near the bottom of this page.

THOMAS POTS, son of Thomas Pots, first pastor of the English Church at Vlissingen, later of the church at Amsterdam, where he died in 1635, and of Sarah de Maayd, was pastor, first, at Vlissingen, then, in 1651, of the English congregation at Utrecht and from November 10, 1654, of the Low Dutch church of the former place.   In September 1684 he came into great inconveniency, because he through great indiscretion had had Koelman, who had been deposed at Sluis, preach for him at Vlissingen, notwithstanding that the States of (Council?) Zeeland had previously forbidden Koelman to preach or to administer the Sacrament in the Province.   On account of this, Pots was summoned before the States (Council?) of Zeeland, but excused himself "because he was suffering from the gout."

The States were (Council was?) not satisfied with this and summoned him anew.   Pots defended himself in the ablest manner and declared he did not know that their resolution in 1674 referred to Koelman, since he (Koelman) had likewise preached for his colleague, Bernardus van Denise.   The consequence of all this was that the two gentlemen were prohibited from preaching for three months and their salaries for that period given to the poor of Vlissingen.

In 1659 he received a call from the English church at Amsterdam, and in 1663 one from the Low Dutch church at Utrecht.   He died in 1689.   From an article written concerning him and spread among the people, it appears that he was not greatly beloved at Vlissingen.   It began thus :—

> "Here lies buried Scottish Tom
> And nobody's sorry for it."

His first wife was Nikoletta Kommersteijn, who died in 1665, and his second Alide de Ruiter, daughter of Admiral M. A. de Ruiter, widow of John Schrorer, an Alderman of Vlissingen.

Page 97.   Below will be found copies of four wills from the Public Record Office at Dublin, Ireland.   The matter

does not seem to show any relationship to the others treated
of, but may, on account of their antiquity and quaintness,
be found of some interest. The original copies have been
followed as closely as possible, but diacritical and other
marks, indicating contractions, have been necessarily omitted

1591   Will of Johannis Potts of Waterford.

In the name of God Amen the xvth of March 1591° I John Potts of
the Cittie of Waterford physicion being sicke in body but of sound
and pfect memorie God be praised do make and ordeine this my last
will and testament in manner and forme following ffirst I gyve and bequeath my soule to Jesus Christ my Saviour and redeemer and my
body to be buried in St John is chappell within Christ is Church in
Waterforde Item I gyve and bequeath to my wife Anstace Dobbin
the lease of farm of Culley to have and enjoy the same during her nat-
urall lyf and after her decease my will is that Edward Madden my
wyfs sonn shall have the posession thereof during the term of yeares
in the saide lease from such tyme uuexpired   Item I gyve and bequeath to the M^t. brethren and poore peopill of the hospitall of the
Holye Ghost in Waterford the somme of xl^s sterling yearly to be paide
to them out of the saide farme during the yeares in the lease comprised   Item wheare theare are certain sommes of monney dew unto
me on Mr Cantwell of the Countie of Kilkeny my will is that my executors according to thear good discretion shall gyve and bestowe
ether the whole or some pt thearof to Joan the sister of the saide M^r.
Cantwell who for a long tyme hath done me trew and faithfull service
Item I gyve and bequeath the fortie pounds ster wch Mrs Ellis Butler
widow oweth me to my wyfe Anstace and her iii sonnes to be divided
betweene them in manner following viz : to my wife the somme xx^{iss}
mcks to Edward Madden her sonn xx^{tie} mcks more Patricke Madden an other xx^{tie} nobles and to James Madden xx^{tie} nobles

Item the rest of all my goods and chattels not gyven nor bequeathed
I do gyve and bequeath to my above named wyfe and to Edward
Madden whom I do nominate and appoint to be my true and sole exee-
utors of this my last will and testament as also Mr Robt Walsh fitz Peter and Mr Walter Graunte overseers of the same these being witnesses William Lamcon Patricke Graunte Pers Graunte Richard Wall
Catherine Dobbin William Lincoll fitz Andrew Thomas White

1626   Will of John Potts of Cannicourt.

M$^{d'}$ that the 7th day of November or thereabouts in the yeere 1625
John Potts of Cannicourt in the Countie of Kildare gentl' beinge of
pfect minde and memorie made his last will and testament nuncupa-

tive in manner and forme followinge vizt first he commended his soule to God Almightie and his boddie to be buried att Newabbey where his former wife was buried and alsoe he lefte to his welbeloved wife Gen Greames als Potts his lease and interest of the farme of Canuicourt duringe the time and tearme comprised in the said lease soly unto her selfe and the rest of his goods and chattles to be devided betwixt her and her children after the paiment of his depts and legacies /

Probat' et approbatu fuit humoi testu nuncupatiou dicit' Johannis Potts defuncti in coi Juris forma actisq Curie Regie Prerogative pro cais ecetics etc' insinuatu et ad' om' et singulor' bonor' juriu creditor' et cattellor' dci defuncti habents &c comissa fuit secund' tubulas testamentarias pd' Jennette Greames als Potts vid' relcct' et Anne Elizabethe Jape et Thome Potts libris dci defucti in psona dci Jennette Potts jurat' p Rs^{ma} in Christo patrem ac dum dm Jacobu providen' dina Armachan Archicpu totius hibnie primat' et Metro^{nn} necnon Judicem psidem sive Comissar' Curie pd' salvo jure cujuseng nono die mensis ffebr' 1626 etils Angelie &c subsignat' p Magros Henricu Maynwaringe in artibus mgiu et Willimu Hilton jurispit' armigeros substitutos dict' Curie Prerogative pro Inventario secunda sessione Termini Pache prox'

1670. Will of Richard Potts, who died at Percival, Scotland.

The testament and lattir will of Richart pottis seck in bodie and haill in mynde Gievin wpe w' his awne mrowthe in his dwelling hous in Wthturture upo ye 28 Day of m'che 1644 yeris Before this witnes Andr coward elder burgis of Stunnawr

Inventar'

In Prms one hundethe Punds starling of redy money   Ite mair aucht hundethe and fowrtie mks In redy money   Ite mair fyve hundeth mks of ye qw Io^n m'caus cozen is awne thrie hundethe mks wa^m moore maltmane one hundethe mks c'forme to yar bonnd   Ite be Iam[ ] m^{c}kittricke in Glenlute one hundethe mks qw copleatis ye sd fyve hundrethe mks   Ite be wa^m Pottis my sonne yatt he tuik w' him of myn to Ireland twenty Punds starling   Ite in Ireland aucht guyes and fowr kuy mair other two kuy and Two stirkes   Ite ane black hors worth fowr Punds starling   Ite in stotland nyne kuy   Ite sex hodges Ite ane Littill black meir   Ite in awing be David Irvein sotyme in airland and nowe in Dufries nyne hundethe mks stots   Ite be Io^n m^{c}caig in port pattrik iiij li

Debtis awing be ye deid

In Prms In awing to Gilbert Damster in Ireland xx li stots   mair to ye sd Gilbert Damster xxv sh' starling

Legasies

In prms I Leave my wyff Jennett Demster auchtein hundeth mks
and noinattis hir my exex   Ite I leave to wa^m pottis my sonne fyve
hundethe mks w' two hundethe mks yatt he has in his awne hand
Ite I leave Jennett and Isobell pottis ye nyne hundethe mks yatt David Irvein is awing me   I leave to Richart Robert Grissall and marga-
ri t pottis my barins to ilk ane of the' thrie hundethe mks   Ite I leave
to bessie pottis thrie Cuy *   This was done Day Place monethe and
yere of god above writtin   Before this witness'   Robert Neisbitt in
wthturlure   Iams kennedy factor to ye [   ] of Cassles and ye sd
Andr' coald

Ita est Gilbert Moore not'us publicus ad premiss requisitus
Robert nisbit witnes
Iames kennedy witnes

1723. Will of Ann Potts, widow, of Drogheda.

In The name of God amen I Ann Potts of Droghedah widdow being
sick & weak in body but of perfect sense & memory praise be given to
Almighty God doe make & ordain This my Last will & Testument in
Manner & form following   First I commend my soul to The hands of
the Almighty God hopeing through the Merits Death & Passion of my
Saviour Jesus Christ to have free pardon & full remission of my Sins
& to inheritt everlasting Life & my body I Committ to The Earth to
be Decently buried according to The Will of my Ex^{rs} hereafter named
Item I will that my Debts & funerall Expenses be first Paid & Dis-
charged   Item I leave and bequeath to my Daughter Elizabeth Potts
The sume of Eighty Pounds sterl'   Item I Leave & bequeath to my
Daughter Mary Potts the Sume of sixty pounds sterl'   Item I Leave
& bequeath my youngest Daughter Ann Potts The sume of sixty
Pounds sterl' to be reced by them severally & Imediately after my
Death   Item my Will is that my said Daughters Doe severally & ppor-
tionably out of their said sev^{ll} Legacies supply & keep my son Bar-
tholemew Potts in apparell During his apprenticeship   Item I bequeath to my son William Potts one mourning Ring vallue twenty
shillings & to my son Norris Potts one other mourning ring vallue
Twenty shill* to be given Them Imediately after my Death   Item my
will is that all other my goods & Chattles Debts & Creditts be equally
Devided amongst my said Three Daughters except one Large gold
ring wch I Devise to my Daughter Elizabeth & my will is that if either or any of my said Daughters Dye before they or Either of them
shou'd Happen to marry that the Share Part Legacie & Proporcon of

---

* NOTE. The following memoranda is entered in the margin, "of ye qw Cuy
y^r is twa for ye barns burding [   ]

such Daughter soe Dyeing before Marriage shall goe to The Surviv-
ours of my said Daughters to be Equally Devided amongst such sur-
viveing Daughters Notwithstanding any Gift Seal or Devise What-
soev' & I appoint my said Daughter Elizabeth Potts & Margaret Quin
spinsters Ex's of this my Last will & Testam' revoking all former
Wills by me heretofore made Published or Declared as Wittness my
Hand & Seal This 27th Day of September 1720   ANN POTTS (l.s.)

Signed Sealed and Published in pesence of us Mossom Wye John
Gifford Dor: Wadman

Elizabetha Potts un' Ex'um in Testo suprascripto nominata Iurata
fuit tam de credulitate veritatis quam de debita executione ejused' 28°
Februarie 1723 coram me

MARM COWGHILL

Probatum et approbatum in comui juris forma actisq Curiæ Regiæ
Prærogæ &c' insinuatim fuit hoc Testum Annæ Potts nuper de Drogheda vidua dfta (hentis &c') necnon execuois ejusd et Admrao Bonor
&c' dti dfti concessa fuer' et sunt per Ressm prem Thoman &c' necnon Ind' &c' Elizabetha Potts Filiæ nrali et ltimæ dtae dftae necnon
uni Extrum in dto testo dti dfti noit' et const' prius ad sancta Dei Ev-
ang' psonatr jurat' (Salvo Jure Margarettae Quin alterius Exris in dto
testo dti dfti noiat et const' cum vener' id petitur' necnon Salvo Jure
&c') Dat' Tertio Die Mensis Martii Anno Dni 1723 Et habet pro In-
venrio in vel citra ulfum Diem Mensis Augusti prox' futur'.

PART II.

Page 117.   To the list of the early emigrants to America,
may be added the name of **Richard Potts,** a famous fish-
erman on the coast of Maine, of about 1660.   '' Potts Chan-
nel'' and '' Potts Point '' were named in his honor.   He
is said to have left descendants.

Page 121.   17th line from the top, for '' 1729-30,'' read
'' 1629-30.''

Page 126.   19th line from top.   ADDITIONAL.   Since
this part of the book was printed, Mr. Rae Reisinger, of
Franklin, Penna., has had some further researches made in
Chesterfield Parish Registers, from which it appears that
RICHARD POTT married ANNA, daughter of Godfriedi Ashe,
May 15, 1636.   She was baptized at Chesterfield, February

8, 1617.*   Richard Pott does not seem to have been born at Chesterfield, as there is no record of his baptism in the Parish Registers, and the name of *Pott* or *Potts* has not been found there prior to 1636.   In addition to the information already given, it may be added that there is brass tablet affixed to the north pillar on the west side of the high altar, of the Chesterfield Parish Church, bearing an inscription to the memory of one JOHANNES POTTS who was buried October 10, 1676.

Pages 136-7.   Since these pages were printed, evidence has come to the notice of the compiler showing quite clearly, that Joseph Borden of the deed was none other than Joseph the founder of Bordentown.   As Joseph's children are all accounted for and none was the wife of a Thomas Potts, the term "son-in-law" was used to indicate a relationship not now accorded to this term.   John Borden, an uncle of Joseph, died in 1716, and by his will left lands in New Jersey and Pennsylvania to his daughters Hope and Mary. Mary is alleged to have been born about 1684, and is the only one of John Borden's children who is not clearly accounted for after his decease.   It seems altogether probable that she removed to New Jersey, and that she may have become a member of her cousin Joseph's household, and subsequently, if she became the wife of Thomas Potts, it would be, at that day, not at all improbable that Joseph would speak of Thomas as his son-in-law.

Page 140.   21st line from top.   From deeds it appears that Thomas Potts was a resident of Bucks County, Pennsylvania, as early as 1737   On November 19, 1715, Collin

---

* THE ASHE FAMILY. From researches made, at the instance of Mr. Rae Reisinger, in the Parish Registers of Chesterfield, we are able to give the following concerning the Ashe family.

1 Radus Ashe, Senr., was buried May 9, 1578.
2 Radus Ashe, son of Radi Ashe, was baptized June 12, 1563.
3 Godfriedus Ashe, son of Radi Ashe, was baptized June 12, 1589.   He married Alice Clay January 15, 1616. Godfriedus Ashe, Shoemaker, was buried Jan. 8, 1643, and Alice, his wife, on May 14, 1641.
4 Anna Ashe, daughter of Godfrey and Alice, was baptized February 8, 1617, and married Richard Pott, May 15, 1636.

Macquire, of Mansfield Township, Burlington County, New Jersey, made a conveyance of land to Thomas Potts, of Mansfield. On 3 mo, 28, 1717, Macquire made another conveyance to Potts. On November 24, 1737, "Thomas Potts, of Bucks County, Pennsylvania," sold the land purchased of Macquire to William English, of Burlington Co., New Jersey. The witnesses were Isaac Horner, Thomas Potts and Sarah Potts.

Page 146. 9th line from top, for "Rebecca" read "Ann"

Page 146. 12th line from top. ADDITIONAL.

14 Joseph Folwell,[4] son of William and Ann (Potts) Folwell, was born Sept. 14, 1748, and died at Romulusville, Seneca County, New York, April 3, 1824. He married Ann Boileau, of Hatboro, Pa., April 30, 1767. She was born February 9, 1751, and died July 3, 1829.

CHILDREN OF JOSEPH AND ANN (BOILEAU) FOLWELL.

i   Isaac Folwell, b. Nov. 14, 1770; d. Jan. 10, 1810.
ii Nathan Folwell, b. Oct. 20, 1772; d. April 27, 1821.
iii Elizabeth Folwell, b. May 4, 1775; d. August 2, 1777.
iv John Folwell, b. April 18, 1779; d. October, 1848.
v   Joseph Folwell, b. June 10, 1781; d. June 6, 1860.
vi Nathaniel Folwell, b. July 4, 1783; d. Dec. 22,1839.
vii Sarah W. Folwell, b. Sept. 30, 1785; d. Feb. 27. 1841.
viii William Folwell, b. Oct. 6, 1787; d. Feb. 9, 1870.
ix Rachel Folwell, b. Feb. 28, 1790; d. April 3, 1838.
x   Charlotte L. Folwell, b. Oct. 23, 1792; d. Feb. 16, 1830.

Page 152. Strike out the 10th line from bottom. See foot-note on page 153.

Page 157. 6th line from top. Thomas Potts married Alice Bunting. The Thomas Potts who married Rebecca King has not been identified.

Page 160. **19 Stacy Potts.** The following extract from a letter, dated August 2, 1768, and written by Stacy Potts, is not only interesting, but is confirmatoy of the facts already set forth at length in the account of the descendants of Thomas Potts, (Shield).

Mahlon Stacy who came over to the wilds of America in the Ship called the Shield from Hull, and arrived in December 1678, with a great number of first settlers of New Jersey, among whom was Thomas Potts my predecessor in the male line, which I need not at present pursue, but to return to the said Mahlon Stacy my other great grandfather who had six children called Elizabeth, Mary, Sarah, Ruth, Rebecca and Mahlon, the latter of whom was with Edward Beakes over with you in or about 1716 then a Widower, he died without issue

The daughters married as followeth, Elizabeth to Abel Jenny of whom are a considerable family. Mary married Reuben Pownell who was also at your house, they died childless. Sarah married Joseph Kirkbride and left one son still living with a number of children and some grandchildren. Rebecca married Joshua Wright and left a pretty large family of descendants, and Ruth married William Beakes then a widower who had two sons William and Edmond by a former wife, and by her he had one daughter and two sons, Sarah (who was my mother), Stacy and Nathan. When the said William Beakes my grand father died and his widow married Samuel Atkinson who is still alive, and by whom he had two sons and two daughters still living. My mother married to Thomas Potts Grandson of the aforsaid Thomas Potts by whom she had six children, five of whom are now living two sons and three daughters. My father died in 1742 when we were all very young and my mother 15 years after. My brother named Richard has a wife and several children as also have my sisters Ruth and Mary. My youngest sister Sarah still unmarried, and myself (the eldest) have been married and have four children, but have had the misfortune to lose my wife about three months past.

Page 162. 3d line from bottom. RUTH POTTS married, first, William Johntson in 1759, and had children as follows;

  i Sarah Johnson, m. Thomas Matthews.
  ii Thomas P. Johnson, m. Mary Stockton.
  iii Samuel Johnson.
  iv William Johnson, d. y.
  v Ruth Johnson, m. Timothy Paxton.

Page 169. The following is a more accurate statement of the children of Stacy an Mary (Sommer) Potts.

CHILDREN OF STACY AND MARY (SOMMER) POTTS.

118 Charles Potts, m. Jane Bordley.
119 Mary Ann Potts, m. George W. Steever.
120 Maria Potts, m. William Evans.

125　Rachel Potts, m. George H. Duhring.
121　Emma Potts, m. James Willis.
124　Esther Potts.
122　Sarah Potts, m. Robert C. Thomson.
　　　Harriet Potts.
123　Albert Potts, m. Emma F. Snyder.

Page 176. ADDITIONAL. Insert and substitute the following.

119　Mary Ann Potts,[6] (Stacy,[5] Stacy,[4] Thomas,[3] Thomas,[2] Thomas,[1] Richard,[*]) daughter of Stacy and Mary (Sommer) Potts, married George W. Steever.

CHILDREN OF GEORGE W. AND MARY ANN (POTTS) STEEVER.

William Steever.　　　Mary Steever, m. Dr. Thomas Corson.
Anna Steever.　　　　Emma Steever, m. Alexander Priestley.
George Steever.　　.　Caroline Steever, m. Alex. Priestley.

123　Albert Potts,[6] (Stacy,[5] Stacy,[4] Thomas,[3] Thomas,[2] Thomas,[1] Richard,[*]), son of Stacy and Mary (Sommer) Potts, married Emma F. Snyder.

CHILDREN OF ALBERT AND EMMA F. (SNYDER) POTTS.

200　Stacy Potts, m. Georgiana R. Smith.
201　Adele Marie Potts.
202　Newton Murray Potts.

125　Rachel Potts,[6] (Stacy,[5] Stacy,[4] Thomas,[3] Thomas,[2] Thomas,[1] Richard,[*]), daughter of Stacy and Mary (Sommer) Potts, married Dr. George H. Duhring.

CHILDREN OF DR. GEORGE H. AND RACHEL (POTTS) DUHRING.

Herman Duhring, m. Lucy Bryant.
Caroline Duhring.
Charles Albert Duhring, m. Sarah Moore.

200　Stacy Potts,[7] (Albert,[6] Stacy,[5] Stacy,[4] Thomas,[3] Thomas,[2] Thomas,[1] Richard,[*]), son of Albert and Emma F. (Snyder) Potts, married Georgiana R. Smith.

CHILDREN OF STACY AND GEORGIANA R. (SMITH) POTTS.

Marion Emma Potts.
Ruth Adele Potts.
Georgiana Rachel Potts.

A Pedigree of Stacy Potts' Family—Ancestors and Descendants

Richard Potts=Anne Ashe

Thomas Potts=Joani

Thomas Potts=Mary Records

Thomas Potts=Sarah Beakes

Stacy Potts=Margaretta Yardley

STACY POTTS=Mary Sommer

No. 58, page 169.
HISTORICAL COLLECTIONS
of the
POTTS FAMILY

—Charles Potts=Jane Bordley——

—Mary Ann=George W. Steever—

—Rachel = Dr. Geo. H. Duhring—

—Maria = William Evans

—Emma = James Willis

—Esther Potts

—Sarah = Robert C. Thomson

—Harriet Potts

—Albert = Emma F. Snyder——

—Mary Potts = James O'Hara
—Emma Potts
—Charles Potts
—B. Bordley Potts = Theresa Rapp

—William Steever
—Anna Steever
—George Steever
—Mary = Dr. Thomas Corson
—Emma = Alex. Priestly
—Caroline = Alex. Priestly

—Herman Louis = Lucy Bryant

—Charles Henry Duhring
—Caroline Adelaide Duhring
—Charles Albert=Sarah Moore—

—Stacy=Georgiana R. Smith——
—Adele Marie Potts
—Newton Murray Potts

—Herman Louis Duhring
—George Henry Duhring
—Joseph Bryant Duhring
—Rachel Ashton Duhring
—Lucy Bryant Duhring
—Emily Bryant Duhring
—Caroline Adelaide Duhring
—George Thomas Duhring
—Rebecca Cecelia Duhring

—Ella Swift Duhring
—Fannie Louise Duhring
—Charles Albert Duhring
—Mabel Moore Duhring
—James L. M. Duhring
—Edwin Leslie Duhring

—Marion Emma Potts
—Ruth Adele Potts
—Georgiana Rachel Potts

Page 178. 11th line from top. Major William Potts was born October 18, 1759. He married, first, ———— Talman; and second, ———— West. He was of the Middlesex family. See page 185.

Page 179. 7th line from top, for "**39**" read "**147**"

Page 196. ADDITIONAL. In 1684, Edmund Bennett was a Member of Assembly from Bucks County ; and on April 6, 1685, he was appointed a Justice of the Peace for Bucks County.

Page 204. 16th line from top, for "1617" read "1717"

Page 215. **8 Jasper Potts.** See page 434, et seq.

Page 217. 7th line from bottom, for "1723" read "1823"

Page 220 et seq. **Jonas Potts.** The following memoranda concerning Jonas Potts has been culled from the records of the old Germantown Court.

Dec. 9, 1701. Jonas Potts was Sheriff.

11 mo. 20, 1701. The Sheriff, Jonas Potts, gave Abraham op de Graeff the lie, for saying that the said Sheriff agreed with Matthew Peters to take his fees 7s and 6d, which upon acknowledgment was forgiven and laid by.

Sept. 15, 1702. Jonas Potts, plaintiff, against Lodovic Christian Sprogle, defendant, being called and not appearing was nonsuited.

4 mo 13, 1704. Jonas Potts was attested to serve as constable, to serve the office as constable for half a year, or until he be equally discharged thereof.

6 mo. 8, 1704. A recognizance wherein Jonas Potts, David Potts and Jacob Shoemaker were bound in the sum of three hundred pounds for the personal appearing of the same Jonas Potts at this court, for having dangerously hurt one William Robinson, &c., was read; and forasmuch as the said Jonas Potts did appear, and nothing was objected against him, in this manner the said Robinson being past all danger of his wounds, he the said Jonas Potts was cleared by proclamation

Oct. 3, 1704. Jonas Potts was a juror. On the same day George Lowther, the Queen's Attorney, brought an indictment against Jonas Potts, to whom the Court answered that it came too late, he the said Potts having been cleared at a former Court of Record.

90

Dec. 1, 1705. At a Court held, Jonas Potts was Coroner.

1 mo. 12, 1705-6. Jonas Potts served as a juror.

Dec. 2, 1706. Jonas Potts was the Sheriff.

Page 226. 17th line from top, and 8th line from bottom, for " Elizabeth Jane ——," read " Elizabeth Lane " See page 291.

Page 235. 15th line from bottom, for " non-cupative " read " nuncupative "

Page 263. 5th line from top, for " 1708 " read " 1709 "

Page 267. ADDITIONAL. 13th line from bottom.

6 Thomas Potts, son of Jonathan and Sarah (Wright) Potts, was born July 19, 1794. Occupation, blacksmith. He married, first, Jane McCullough, about 1817. After her decease, he married, second, Cynthia Whiteside, in 1841. The descendants reside in New Castle County, Delaware.

CHILDREN OF THOMAS AND JANE (McCULLOUGH) POTTS

11 William Potts. He married, settled about North East, Maryland, and left several children.

12 A daughter who married Joseph Dawson and left 7 children.

13 A daughter who married William Ferguson and left 7 children.

CHILDREN OF THOMAS AND CYNTHIA (WHITESIDE) POTTS.

14 David Potts, m. Sarah Shepard.

15 Thomas Addison Potts, b. Oct. 31, 1847; m. Rebecca Ford.

16 Robert Gibson Potts, m. Mary Scanlon.

17 George G. Potts, m. Sarah Hendrickson.

18 Mary Potts, m. James Crosson.

19 Granville Potts, m. Emma Dalton.

20 Louis Potts, m. Anna Hendrickson.

15 Thomas Addison Potts,[3] son of Thomas an Cynthia (Whiteside) Potts, was born Oct. 31, 1847. He is a manufacturer of Scotch snuff, and has been in the employ of Garrett & Sons for more than thirty years. He married Rebecca Ford, May 4, 1871. Residence, Hockessin, New Castle County, Delaware.

CHILDREN OF THOMAS A. AND REBECCA (FORD) POTTS.

21 Frank Potts.
22 Lawrence Potts.
23 Calvin Potts.
24 Cora Potts.

25 Ralph Potts.
26 Lena Potts.
27 Mary Elizabeth Potts.

Page 295. Below is a fair copy of the signature of Jonas Potts, as it appears attached to his will on file at Leesburg, Virginia.

Page 295. 22d line from top, for "1769" read "1768"

Page 306. Below is a fuller record of the children and grandchildren of Edwin H. and Jane (Clendenning) Potts.

100 William C. Potts, b. June 12, 1845; m. Sarah E. Reed. Chil-
   1 Walter L., 2 Robertie, 3 Clarence H.

101 Emma I. Potts, b. October 10, 1846; m. Matthias P. Zacharias.
   He died August 1, 1882. Child, Clara J.

99 Ruth Ellen Potts, b. May 2, 1848; d. September 7, 1853.

102 Walter B. Potts, b. Nov. 4, 1849; m. Anna M. Shriver, who died
   Oct. 24, 1884. Child, Edwin H.

103 Sarah E. Potts, b. August 10, 1851; m. David Conard Neer.
   Children, 1 Jessie J., 2 Mabel E., 5 Nathan N., 4 Edwin H.

104 Laura A. Potts, b. August 30, 1853; m. Samuel O. Clendenning.
   Child, Nellie.

105 Edwin Clinton Potts, b. August 17, 1855; m. Laura Virginia
   James. Children, 1 Hazel E., 2 Bertha J., 3 Thurston J., 4
   F. Jennings, 5 L. Virginia.

106 Harry Clay Potts, b. Feb. 3, 1857; m. Lizzie Beans. Children,
   1 Blanche M., 2 Ruth H., 3 E. Humphrey, 4 L. Russell, 5
   Ethel B., 6 Clara E.

107 Nathaniel D. Potts, b. April 20, 1859; m. Martha Gregory.

108 Eppa Hunter Potts, b. Feb. 1, 1861; m. Sallie Bet Gregory.
   Children, 1 Mildred, 2 Laura Amanda.

Page 314. 3d and 13the lines from top, for "1742" read "1757"

Page 314. 2 David Potts. The following are copies of the inscriptions on the tombstones of David Potts and his wife, in the old graveyard at Marion, Ohio, kindly furnished by Mr. Henry True of that city. This shows that David Potts was born about the year 1757.

In Memory of | David Potts | who died May 27th, 1837 | Aged 80 years.

In Memory of | PERMILLA POTTS | who died June 15, 1833 | Aged 72 years.

Page 315. 16th line from top. DAVID POTTS. Some information has been received from Mrs. Adaline Potts Graham, of Huntingdon, Baker County, Oregon, who is a granddaughter of one David Potts, who may be identical with the above David, though not positively proven. Mrs. Graham says that her grandfather, David Potts, was born in Loudoun County, Virginia, and had children, 1 JONAS, 2 ANDREW, 3 SARAH, 4 ELIZABETH. Jonas Potts was born about 1813. He married Annie Hutton at Marlborough, Stark County, Ohio, and continued to reside there until about 1875, when he removed to Davis County, Missouri. The children of Jonas Potts were 1 Adaline, 2 Marian, 3 Elizabeth, 4 Dora. This family claimed to be cousins of the late Gen. B. F. Potts, sometime Governor of Montana.

Page 332. 123. **William Jackson Potts** was born on August 24, 1814. Margaret Ward Potts, his wife, died on September 1, 1900.

Page 361. 12th line from top, for "December 1," read "December 10," George Murdock Potts, son of George Dunlap and Rose Frances (Greenan) Potts, was born September 20, 1900.

Page 361. 2d line from the bottom, for "Mamie" read "Minnie"

Page 367. The statement of Dr. Rockwell, printed in the paragraph near the bottom of this page, as to the children of William Potts, is probably inaccurate.

Page 382. 16th line from top. **13 Henry Potts.** ADDITIONAL. Miss Ella Potts, of Sylva, North Carolina, has furnished the compiler with a fuller account of Henry Potts

and his descendants, of which the following is a brief abstract.
HENRY POTTS,[4] son of James and Sarah (Tinon) Potts, was
born about 1766, and died February 2, 1850. He married
Margaret Henry about 1798, in Iredell County, North Carolina. She was born about 1780, and died May 28, 1843.
They resided near Statesville, until 1828, when they removed, first, to Waynesville, Haywood County, and subsequently to Jackson County. Occupation, farmer. Place of
burial, East Laporte, Jackson County, North Carolina.

CHILDREN OF HENRY AND MARGARET (HENRY) POTTS.

i   Sarah Tinon Potts, b. Oct. 10, 1799; d. May 30, 1888; unm.
ii Esther Stewart Potts, b. Sept. 9, 1802; d. Feb. 19, 1890; unm.
iii James Henderson Potts, b. Dec. 28, 1804; m. Catharine Slate.
    Children, 1 Margaret, m. —— Brown; 2 Jane, m. Lanson
    Brown; 3 Ann, m. James Hooper; 4 John; 5 William, m. Ta-
    bitha Dills; 6 Sarah; 7 Eva.
iv Wilson Potts, m. Margaret Allison. Children, 1 Margaret, m.
    Marion Dills; 2 Malinda; 3 Jane; 4 Mary, m. William Frank-
    lin; 5 Sarah, m. Houston Bryson; 6 Rufus, m. Ellen Mundy;
    7 Callie, m. Clark McDade.
v   Lanson Potts, b. 1814; d. March 22, 1891; m. Evie Davidson.
    Children, 1 Margaret, 2 Catharine, 3 Emeline. 4 Missouri, 5
    Francis Lee.
vi Eunice (called Nicely) Potts, m. John Brown. Children, 1 Sa-
    rah, 2 Melissa, 3 Rebecca, 4 Elbert, 5 Jesse, 6 Pilgrin.
vii Evaline Potts. b. ——; d. October 23, 1869; m. Frank Allison.
    Children, 1 Catharine, 2 Sam, 3 Rufus.
viii John Lee Potts, b. August 12, 1818; d. Nov. 6, 1897; m. Hattie
    Ripley, 1868. Children, 1 Margaret Narcissa, 2 Ella, 3 Lela.

Page 388. 12th line from top. ADDITIONAL. William
A. Potts,[6] son of James M. and Nannie C. (Torrence) Potts,
born Jan. 3, 1866, married Lucy S. Thompson, daughter of
Samuel and Lettie M. (Asbury) Thompson, Feb. 3, 1887.
She was born Oct. 14, 1870. Occupation, farmer and mer-
chant. Residence, Davidson, Mecklenburg County, N. C.

CHILDREN OF WILLIAM A. AND LUCY S. (THOMPSON) POTTS.

i   Cloyd Alexander Potts, b. Dec. 25, 1887.
ii William Marshall Potts, b. January 29, 1890.
iii Samuel Monroe Potts, b. October 26, 1891.
iv Louis Potts, b. September 2, 1893.
v   Madge Wayland Potts, b. March 12, 1895.

vi Katharine Potts, b. March 20, 1897.
vii Mary Winifred Potts, b. December 13, 1898.

Page 421. 5th line from the top. George Potts married *Margaret* McKeever.

PART III.

Page 442. 3d line from top, for "Agnes" read "Alice"

Page 454. 11th line from top, for "1695" read "1721"

Page 454. 22d line from top, for "1717" read "1729"

Page 457. 11th line from top, erase "d. Sept. 9, 1746." Sarah Potts seems to have been still living in 1768, when Joseph Potts (28) mentions "my Sister" in his will.

Page 457. 12th line from top, for "11" read "10"

Page 462. 11th line from top, for "Hugh Hughes Potts" read "Hugh Henry Potts"

Page 462. 6th line from bottom, for "hoseltries" read "hostelries"

Page 467. 6th line from top. The will of Joseph Potts is recorded at Philadelphia, in Will-Book O, page 497. He makes bequests to "my loving Mother," to "my Brother William," to "my Sister," to "my wife's mother," and to my "Loving Wife Meriam Potts."

Page 467. 20th line from top. Esther, sometimes called Hester, wife of William B. Potts, was a daughter of Stacy and Sarah Moore. William B. Potts died about 1808, as letters of administration were granted "unto Isaac White on the Estate of William B. Potts, mariner, deceased," on September 14, 1808.

Page 468. 13th line from the bottom, for "1810" read "1816"

Page 472. 3d line from bottom, for "Robert Trotter Potts" read "Robert Tower Potts."

Page 475. 7th line from the top, for " Mary Joy" read " Mary Joy Ridgway."

Page 475. 12th line from top. **56 Hugh Henry Potts.** The following extract from a letter written to the compiler in 1885, by the late William John Potts, concerning Hugh Henry Potts and others of that connection, contains interesting matter worth preserving.

This summer I have renewed my acquaintance with Mr. George H. Potts, of the City of New York, above spoken of. He is, as you are aware, first cousin to my father and is now seventy four years old, a tall, distinguished and elegant looking man of at least six feet high, not inclined to stoutness which characterizes two of his sons. * *

Among Mr. George H. Potts' traditions of his father, uncles, and grandfather were several which were confirmed in part by my aunt (Hannah) Elizabeth Potts and my uncle Charles Clay Potts, both aged above seventy years. Hugh Potts, as he was commonly called, though his full name was Alexander Hugh, father of the said George, and brother to my grandfather, was a remarkably handsome man. One of the Robesons who had known him in his youth, possibly an old sweetheart of his, said he was the handsomest man she ever knew. The said Mary Robeson died in Philadelphia aged above seventy years ten or more years ago.

Hugh Potts was six feet one inch high, weighed 220 pounds and was a most powerful man. On one occasion he lifted with one hand fourteen (14) fifty six (56) pound weights to above the knee. He held on his outstretched hand, one Ramsay, Sheriff of Hunterdon County, in a standing position, he being steadied by a man on each side of him, took him entirely across the room. He also carried the said Ramsay standing on his (Mr. Potts') knee, the back part of it turned up, across the room. Mrs. Rockhill, sister to Hugh Potts, was also of large frame. She was six feet in height. * * *

Thomas Potts, High Sheriff of Sussex County, N. J., [father of Hugh Potts,] on one occasion had to arrest Edward Marshall, the hero of the famous Indian walk, who lived on an island in the Delaware out of his jurisdiction, and was beside no mean adversary. My great grandfather Thomas Potts, a large and powerful man, took a boat and crossing over to the island where Marshall lived, bound him hand and foot and when he landed his prisoner on the Jersey shore, served his warrant on him.

Page 477. **60 Jesse Potts.** He was a Friend or Quaker, and a member of the Masonic fraternity. A gold Masonic emblem, bearing date of 1808, is now in possession of his grandson, Jesse Walker Potts, of Albany. He seems to have been a man of taste and more than ordinary education. Many of his books, some fine pieces of furniture, and a fine old "grandfather's clock," are preserved by the grandson above named.

Page 482.   11th line from the bottom, Isaac Jones died March 14, 1811.

Page 492,   13th line from top, for "1810" read "1800"

Page 494.   11th line from top, Jane Mather died July 23, 1897.

Page 494.   8th line from bottom, for "Robert Trotter Potts" read "Robert Tower Potts"

Page 504.   The following is an abstract of the chain of title to the homestead farm of the late Thomas Jefferson Potts and later of William Potts, situate in Highland Township, Chester County, Pennsylvania.

1681.   Letters Patent, of King Charles, II, to William Penn for the Province of Pennsylvania.

1681.   William Penn, Proprietor of the Province of Pennsylvania, to Thomas Dell, of Upton in the County of Bucks, England, 500 acres.

1711.   Thomas Dell, the elder, then of Kensington, County Middlesex, England, to Thomas Dell, the younger, of Chester County, Pennsylvania, 500 acres.

1713–4. Warrant granted to the son Thomas Dell for 500 acres.

1724.   Thomas Dell, the younger, of Ridley Township, Chester County, to John Stringer, for 265 acres, part of the original 500.

1737.   John Stringer died intestate, leaving a wife Martha, and issue Joseph George, Daniel, William, Sarah, and Martha intermarried with Daniel Nichols, and letters of administration were granted to the son William Stringer.

1750.   Joseph Stringer, et al., heirs of John Stringer, deceased, to William Stringer, 143 acres, part of the 265 acres, being in the southwest corner of the original grant of 500 acres.

1783. William Stringer died, leaving a will, in which he mentions wife Esther, deceased, and children John, William, George, Elinor, Martha, and Sarah, intermarried with David McKim. He left the said farm to son William.

1807. William Stringer, (Junior), late of West Fallowfield, now of the State of Ohio, to James Hollis, of West Fallowfield, 143 acres.

1808. Patent from the Commonwealth of Pennsylvania to James Hollis, for 143 acres. The Warrant of 1713-4, and the sundry other conveyances are all recited.

1812. James Hollis and wife to James W. Potts, 143 acres.

1825. Jesse Sharp, Sheriff of Chester County, to Thomas Jefferson Potts, 143 acres.

Page 522. 15th line from bottom, for "**347**" read "**348**"

Page 535. **433 Anna T. Potts.** Mrs. Anna T. (Potts) Jones, of Conshohocken, Penna., died October 19, 1900

Page 536. 3d line from bottom, for "1837" read "1838"

Page 551. To the children of Alfred Hamilton Potts add the following,
Thomas Alva Potts, b. October 22, 1900.
James Alpha Potts, b. October 22, 1900; d. October 31, 1900.

Page 553. 9th line from top, for "1894,, read "1884"

Page 559. 11th line from bottom. Mrs. Pleasant (Hill) Cleaver died November 2, 1900.

Page 560. 8th line from bottom, for " Mary Norman " read " Harry Norman "

Page 581. 16th line from the top. Rev. Harry Roberts Carson, Rector of the P. E. Church at Franklin, Louisiana, and Miss Zoe Theotiste Garig, were married at St. James P. E. Church, Baton Rouge, Louisiana, February 21, 1900.

Page 592. 16th line from the top, for " Frorence " read " Florence"

Page 602. 14th line from top. Mahlon L. Cleaver died November 11th, 1900.

Page 613. 4th line from top, for "Cleaver" read "Espy"

81

Memoranda.

RICHARD POTTS. David McKown, or McKewen, a merchant of Barbadoes, was for some time in the City of Philadelphia, where he was taken sick and died about the year 1694. His will, dated Dec. 26, 1694, and proven January 7, 1694-5, is recorded in Will-Book, C, page 297, at Philadelphia. He was a man of considerable estate. He names his wife Ann, and mentions, *inter alia,* his ''silver headed cane,'' and £44, 16s., and a hundred weight of tobacco, in the hands of Richard Potts. At the probating of the will, Richard Potts made oath that '' he did write y* Last Will & Testament within mentioned by y* speciall direction of the wthin named david M^{ac}Kowine.'' Richard Potts was named as one of the executors. A loose paper filed with the original will, in a handwriting other, than that of Richard Potts, is a renunciation of executorship of the said Richard Potts, but it is unsigned. This Richard Potts has not been identified, and it is possible that he was only temporarially in this country.

THOMAS POTTS. The ''Annals of the Shotwell Family,'' contains the record of the marriage of Abraham Shotwell, (b. 1719), son of John, Jr., and Mary (Thorne) Shotwell, of Shotwell's Landing, on the Rahway River, in Essex [now Union] County, New Jersey, and Mary Potts, daughter of Thomas and Phebe Potts, of '' Honey Neck, Conattecut,'' in 1742. They were Friends and passed Meeting on 9 mo. 4, the second time. Mary (Potts) Shotwell died 3mo. 31, 1762. No further information of this family of Potts has been found and no such place as '' Honey Neck '' is known in the state of Connecticut at this time.

The three persons mentioned below, each bearing the name of John Potts, have not been identified, but they may have belonged to some of the families heretofore recorded.

JOHN POTTS. In 1744, one John Potts was registered in Pennsylvania as an Indian Trader.

JOHN POTTS. On May 1, 1759, John Potts was Ensign in the Military Company of Captain Richard Gardner, of Pennsylvania.

JOHN POTTS. Among those who accompanied the Lewis and Clark exploring expedition to the Rocky Mountains, in 1804-5, was one John Potts. During the expedition, Potts and one Colter obtained permission to stop for the purpose of trapping and hunting, intending shortly to overtake the main body. As there had been a recent encounter with the Blackfeet Indians, the trappers were aware that extreme caution was necessary to escape the vengence of the Indians.

Their plan of operation was to set their traps in the evening, visit them early in the morning and remain in hiding during the day. One morning while rowing up stream a heavy tramping was heard. Colter declared it to be the approach of Indians and was for taking to flight at once, but Potts laughed at him, declaring that the sound was that of a herd of buffaloes, and kept ahead. It was but a short time until both banks of the stream were lined with Indians. As there was no possible chance of escape, they obeyed the command to row to shore, where they were at once surrounded by the savage Blackfeet. Just as they stepped ashore, a burly Indian snatched Potts' rifle, but Colter, being a man of great strength, wrested it from him and returned it to Potts, who jumped into the canoe and pushed out into the stream. Colter called to Potts to come ashore, but he kept out into the current and soon called out. "Colter, I am wounded." Colter turned and saw the Indian who had shot Potts just taking down his bow, and while looking at him he heard Potts' rifle and saw the Indian drop dead   A moment later, Potts' lifeless body fell into the canoe, pierced by hundreds of arrows. Colter was subsequently given a chance of life by running and succeeded in escaping. Washington Irving, Bradbury and others have written graphic accounts of this thrilling affair.

THOMAS POTTS. Thomas Potts, who was sometime Governor of British Honduras, was a man of great wealth and held large possessions in Honduras, and had funds invested in both England and the United States. He died about October, 1806. His wife, Catharine Ferara, belonged to one of the chief families of Honduras. His will is lengthy and disposes of a large amount of property to many different individuals. He mentions his brothers Richard and James of London, England, his sister Elizabeth, his son James Potts, his son Robert Potts then in New York, his son John Potts then in Leipsic, Germany, his daughter Mary Potts then in London, and his daughter Anna Grace Potts. He also mentions his nephew Richard Potts son of his brother James, his nephew John Potts, his cousin Frances Pendergrast, and many others in which no relationship is mentioned. Robert Potts, the son, seems to have left descendants in this country. One of his daughters married that John Redman Coxe, who was born in 1799, and was living a widow in Philadelphia as late as 1890.

ROBERT POTTS. One Robert Potts came from Ireland to Pennsylvania about the year 1824. After spending some time among friends in Huntingdon County, he removed to the western part of the State and settled in Beaver County. Here he engaged in farming and died there in 1851. The traditions of the family allege that their ancestors came into Ireland from Scotland. Robert Potts' wife's name was Eliza, and his children were Robert, Samuel, Charles, John, David and Margaret. John Potts, the son, continued to reside in Beaver County, and at last account he was still living, a highly respected citizen, at above eighty years of age. David Potts, son of Robert, Junior, resides at Washington, Pennsylvania.

An Anglo-Hibernian Potts Family.

Just before sending the last pages of this work to press, some information came to hand concerning a family of Potts of English origin who settled in County Cavan, Ireland, and later in America. This information has been furnished by Dr. George J. Potts, now of Victoria, British Columbia. It came too late to gather other details or trace a more remote ancestry. This family has occupied a high social position. Of the early history of the family, Doctor Potts gives only what he learned from his seniors while he was yet a boy. The family claimed a lineage running back for more than four hundred years. It is possible that this hastily prepared sketch may contain some inaccuracies, but it may prove a basis for a fuller pedigree.

1 JOHN POTTS,[1] a native of England, is supposed to have been born in either Cheshire or Derbyshire. He served as an officer of some rank in the British Army, and was in Egypt under Sir Ralph Abercrombie at the time of the first Bonaprarte War. While still in the Army, he married Miss Jeanette Tought, or Tout, the daughter of a Presbyterian minister of Dundee or Aberdeen, Scotland. He accompanied the Army into Ireland, and when the troubles were over, retired from it on full pay and took up his residence at Drumislady, County Cavan, Ireland. At his death he was buried in the graveyard of Kildalon Church. The upright tombstone still remains. His widow survived him for several years and received a pension from the English government.

Dr. Potts says he well remembers his grandfather's house at Drumislady, a long structure, partly built of stone. The dwelling part was one and a half stories high, with wings one story high, built with old style mortar walls and covered with a straw thatched roof. The stable, cow house, etc., were at one extreme end, the whole structure being perhaps two hundred or more feet in length. The Parish Church and graveyard of Kilnagher, surrounded by a stone high wall, stood about two hundred yards in front of the house.

Dr. Potts states that two brothers of his grandfather, John Potts, served in the army under Gen. Washington and that eventually one or both settled at or about Philadelphia, Pa.

CHILDREN OF JOHN AND JEANETTE (TOUGHT) POTTS.

2 Alexander Potts, b. 1786; d. 1852; m. Jane Lovat.
3 William Potts, d.   ; d.   ; m.
4 David Potts.
5 Daniel Potts.
6 Jeany Potts, m. John Thurber.
7 Christiana Potts, m. John Elliott.

2 **Alexander Potts,**[2] (John,[1]), son of John and Jeanette (Tought) Potts, was born 1786, in County Cavan, Ireland. When quite a young man he married Miss Jane Lovat. The Lovats were of Scotch descent, and were connected with the Frasier family. He had the appointmenet as Parish Clerk, and also served as the agent of the Bishop and Clergy of the Diocese of Clogher. He eventualy emigrated to America, landing at New York, and subsequently removing to Ontario. He settled at Belleville, in Hastings County, where he purchased a farm. He was unused to farm life, and exposure brought on Bronchitis, followed by Aphonia, from the effects of which he died December 19, 1852. His wife survived him more than twenty years and died in 1873. Both lie buried at Belleville, in the graveyard of St. Thomas Parish Church, where a monument marks their resting place.

CHILDREN OF ALEXANDER AND JANE (LOVAT) POTTS.

8 John Potts.
9 Alexander Potts.
10 William Lovat Potts, m. Ann Jane Elliott.
11 George Jerald Potts, M. D., m. Agnes Stewart.
12 Charles Robert Potts, M. D.
13 Christiana Potts, m. George Johnston.
14 Marianne Potts, m. William Anderson.
15 Eliza Jane Potts, m. William Watt.

3 **William Potts,**[2] (John,[1]), son of John and Jeanette
(Tought) Potts, was born in County Cavan, Ireland. He
married a half sister of Jane Lovat, his brother Alexander's
wife. They emigrated to Canada in 1844, and settled on a
farm in Hope Township, Durham County, Ontario. He
died at Ancaster, Haldimand County, at above eighty years
of age. He was a man of means and independence. He
had several sons and three or four daughters, but the names
of only two sons have been furnished.

CHILDREN OF WILLIAM AND ——— (———) POTTS.

16 Henry Potts.
17 Charles David Potts.

4 and 5 **David Potts**[2] and **Daniel Potts,**[2] (John,[1]),
sons of John and Jeanette (Tought) Potts, are said to have
to have emigrated to America and settled at or near Philadelphia, Pennsylvania.

6 **Jeany Potts,**[2] (John,[1]), daughter of John and Jeanette
(Tought) Potts, was born in County Cavan, Ireland. She
married John Thurbur. After his death, she remained a
widow and died at an advanced age. She was buried in the
garveyard of Kilnagher Church. They had one son who
entered the Army and was killed in the Battle of Cape
of Good Hope.

7 **Christiana Potts,**[2] (John,[1]), daughter of John and

Jeanette (Tought) Potts, was born in County Cavan, Ireland. She married James Elliott. They emigrated to Canada, and engaged in farming at Millbrook, County Durham. Ontario, where they became wealthy and acquired large landed possessions. Mr. Elliott died about 1870 to 1875. His wife survived him and died at above seventy years of age. They lie buried at Millbrook. They had a family of four sons and four daughters. The youngest son succeeded to the homestead.

----

8 John Potts,[3] (Alexander,[2] John,[1]), son of Alexander and Jane (Lovat) Potts, was born at Mohr, County Cavan. Ireland. He entered the Army much against his father's desire, and served in India during the Sikh campaign, and in the Cape of Good Hope during the first troubles with the Boers. Lord Gough was his Commander in Chief. After fourteen years of service, his father purchased his discharge and he accompanied the family to Canada. He died suddenly at Ancaster, Ontario, at the age of forty nine years, unmarried.

9 Rev. Alexander Potts,[3] (Alexander,[2] John,[1]), son of Alexander and Jane (Lovat) Potts, was born at Mohr, County Cavan, Ireland. He taught school and studied for the ministry. He became dissatisfied with the unfortunate conditions existing in Ireland, with famine prevailing, and agrarian outrages, frequently accompanied with murder and assassination, he left Ireland, accompanied by his two youngest sisters, Marianne and Eliza Jane, and came to Canada. Their letters home and the mother's desire to be near her children, induced the father to remove with his family to Canada.

Alexander Potts took holy orders, in Canada, and after serving as curate and missionary, was appointed to the Parishes of Delaware and Lambeth adjoining in the Diocese of

Huron, where through his labors a beautiful Brick Church was erected about six miles from London, Ontario. It is alleged that his constant labor and zeal, in connection with the erection of this Church, brought on some trouble with his liver which eventually caused his death in 1865. He was buried within the Church grounds, at the urgent wishes of his congregation, who erected a handsome monument to his memory. He married Miss Elizabeth Courtney who still survives. They had one child, a son, who died at the age of twenty seven years.

10 **William Lovat Potts,**[3] (Alexander,[2] John,[1]), son of Alexander and Jane (Lovat) Potts, was born at Mohr, County Cavan, Ireland. He received a fair education, but his taste inclining to farming, his father sent him at the age of 19 years, to the care of Adam Lucas an old friend, and a planter in the West Indies. He remained in the West Indies until the rest of the family removed to Canada, when he followed them and engaged in farming with great success. He married Ann Jane Elliott, daughter of John an Christiana (Potts) Elliott, a first cousin, by whom he had three children, one son and two daughters.

He retired from farming, entered into mercantile pursuits and failed. He removed with his family to Rochester, New York, where his wife, his son and younger daughter died. He afterward entered the employ of the Pennsylvania Rail Road and removed to Philadelphia, where he died in 1884. His eldest daughter married Mr. ———— Vanever and resides at Omaha, Nebraska.

11 **George Jerald Potts, M. D.,**[3] (Alexander,[2] John,[1]), son of Alexander and Jane (Lovat) Potts, was born at Mohr, County Cavan, Ireland, and when twelve years of age came with his parents to Canada. He was educated at the High School at Belleville, Ontario, and for four years served

82

as a clerk in a general store.   On account of the discovery of gold in Australia, he went to that country and had fair success.   Subsequently·he went to London, England, where he studied medicine, and in 1856 obtained the qualification as M. R. C. S. Eng.   He went to Australia a second time as Medical Superintendent of the Government emigrants to Victoria.   The vessel was chartered for India and the Straits settlements.   Upon arriving at Singapore, learning of a probable vacancy in the Hospital, he applied for the place and received the appointment.   He was appointed as Resident Surgeon in Charge of the East India Company Invalid Hospital with the privilege of private practice.   This position he held for three years, with no little success and popularity.

He was induced to accept the position of Surgeon to her Britanic Majesty's Consul at Bankok, Siam, with greatly increased pay and emoluments.   At the end of eleven months, the mutiny occurred in India, and he with twelve other Consular Surgeons were ordered to Calcutta.   On arriving at Calcutta, they were organized into an Auxilliary Medical Staff Corps, of which Dr. Potts was appointed the Chief Medical Officer or Superintendent.   After the mutiny had been quelled the Corps were ordered to China where the Anglo-French War against the Chinese was about to begin active operations.   At the close of the Chinese War, Dr. Potts resigned his position, at Hong Kong, and returned to America, arriving in New York early in 1861, and was there when Abraham Lincoln passed through the city on his way to Washington to be inaugurated.

The following year, Dr. Potts applied to Surgeon General Hammond, U. S. A., for an appointment as a Surgeon in the U. S. service.   He was ordered to report to the Army Medical Board at Boston for examination, and later recommended to the President for appointment.   He was sworn in on March 12.   He served under General Grant, in the

Army of the Potomac, and was afterward sent to Texas, where he continued until October, 1865. After leaving the U. S. service, he returned to Belleville, Ontario, where he practiced Medicine and Surgery for three years, when he settled at Toronto, where he continued until 1898, and since that time he has resided at Victoria, British Columbia.

Dr. Potts married Miss Agnes Stewart in 1868. She is a lineal descendant of "Annie Laurie," of poetic story, and whose family name was Ferguson of Craig-Darig, Scotland. Their youngest daughter, Jessie, is said to resemble her famous ancestor in features and general appearance.

CHILDREN OF DR. GEORGE J. AND AGNES (STEWART) POTTS.

18 George Alexander Stewart Potts.
19 MacDonald Tupper Potts.
20 Albert Ralph Potts, b. 1879; d. 1898.
21 Murray Clarke Potts.
22 Gerald Cleveland Potts.
23 Helen Electa Finley Potts, m. Henry E. Maxwell.
24 Georgiana Barbara Potts.
25 Jessie Margraita Potts.

12 **Charles Robert Potts, M.D.,[3]** (Alexander,[2] John,[1]) son of Alexander and Jane (Lovat) Potts, was born at Mohr, County Cavan, Ireland, and came with the family to America. He studied Medicine at Queens College, Kingston, Ontario, and graduated with high honor. For sometime he he practiced medicine at Oakwood Mariposa, Victoria County, and later at Robbins Mills, Prince Edward County. He went from there to London, England and received the M. R. C. S. E. Upon his return to Canada, he settled at Tweed, Hastings County, Ontario, where he lost his life by an accident at the early age of twenty nine years. He was buried beside his parents at Belleville.

He married Miss Aggie Haught, of Fredericksburg Ontario, by whom he had three children, one son and two daughters, all living. Aggie, the eldest daughter, married John Sherman, manager of the Hawksbury Lumber Mills, and is now (1901) Mayor of the municipality of Hawksbury, Ontario.

13   **Christiana Potts,**[3] (Alexander,[2] John,[1]) daughter of Alexander and Jane (Lovat) Potts, was born at Mohr, County Cavan, Ireland.   She married George Johnston, who was manager of the Ballyhassie Flour and Corn Mills, County Cavan.   Mr. Johnston died about 1870, and was buried at Ballyhassie.   After her husband's death, Christiana took up her residence with her daughter at Belfast, where she died about 1885.   There were four sons and one daughter Margaret, who married a Mr. Bigger and resides at Belfast.

14   **Marianne Potts,**[3] (Alexander,[2] John,[1]), daughter of Alexander and Jane (Lovat) Potts, was born at Mohr, County Cavan, Ireland.   She removed to Canada with her brother Alexander, and in course of time married William Anderson.   They lived in Prince Edward County, Ontario. Mr. Anderson was twice elected a Member of the Canadian Parliament.   He died suddenly about 1896 or 7.   Marianne, the widow, lives with her youngest son, at the old homestead.   She is enjoying good health at the age of nearly four score years.   There are three sons, all of whom are well-to-do farmers.

15   **Eliza Jane Potts,**[3] (Alexander,[2] John,[1]), daughter of Alexander and Jane (Lovat) Potts, was born at Mohr, County Cavan, Ireland.   She accompanied her brother Alexander and sister Marianne to Canada, where she married William Watt, who died about 1897.   After the death of her brother Charles Robert, she took charge of his two daughters and brought them up.   She now resides with her niece, Mrs. Aggie Sherman, at Hawksbury, Ontorio.

16 **Captain Henry Potts,**[3] (William,[2] John,[1]), son of William Potts, entered the British Army, and after service, retired with honor and on full pay. He resides at Welland, Canada.

17 **Charles David Potts,**[3] (William,[2] John,[1]), son of William Potts, resides a Glanford, Haldimand County, Ontario. In his younger days he taught school, but later engaged in farming with success. He is a gentleman of position and wealth. He was offered for a Member of Parliament for his County and failed of election by only a few votes.

18 **George Alexander Stewart Potts,**[4] (George Jerald,[3] Alexander,[2] John,[1]), son of Dr. George J. and Agnes (Stewart) Potts, was educated at Coburg Collegiate Institute and at Victoria University. Later he went to Victoria, British Columbia, where he studied law, and became a partner in the law firm of Tupper, Peters & Potts. After two years he left the firm and opened an office at Nelson, but subsequently returned to Victoria, where he has a successful practice. He is married and has one daughter.

19 **MacDonald Tupper Potts,**[4] (George Jerald,[3] Alexander,[2] John,[1]), son of Dr. George J. and Agnes (Stewart) Potts, resides at Victoria, British Columbia, where he is the General Manager of the Klondyke Navigation Company.

20 **Albert Ralph Potts,**[4] (George Jerald,[3] Alexander,[2] John,[1]), son of Dr. George J. and Agnes (Stewart) Potts, was educated at Coburg Collegiate Institute and at Jarvis Street Collegiate Institute, Toronto. He successfully passed a law examination at Osgood Hall, Toronto, and articled himself to a leading law firm of that City. He died of Ap-

pendicitis March 14, 1898, at the age of nineteen years.   He was buried in the graveyard of St. James Cathedral, Toronto.

21   **Murray Clarke Potts,**[4] (George Jerald,[3] Alexander,[2] John,[1]), son of Dr. George J. and Agnes (Stewart) Potts, was educated at Jarvis Street Collegiate Institute, Toronto, and took a two years course in practical science in the University of Toronto.   He is now (1901) a student at law in the City Solicitor's Office at Victoria, British Columbia.

22   **Gerald Cleveland Potts,**[4] (George Jerald,[3] Alexander,[2] John,[1]), son of Dr. George J. and Agnes (Stewart) Potts, is now (1901) a student at Church Collegiate Institute, preparing to enter the University of Toronto.

23   **Helen Electa Finley Potts,**[4] (George Jerald,[3] Alexander,[2] John,[1]), eldest daughter of Dr. George J. and Agnes (Stewart) Potts, graduated from Trinity College, Toronto, with the Degree of Bachelor of Arts.   She married Henry E. Maxwell, second son of Judge Maxwell, who was Chief Justice of Nebraska, U. S. A., and later a Member of Congress from that State.   They settled at Omaha, Nebraska, where she died April 17, 1899, within less than a year after her marriage.

24   **Georgiana Barbara Potts,**[4] (George Jerald,[3] Alexander,[2] John,[1]), daughter of Dr. George Jerald and Agnes (Stewart) Potts, graduated from Trinity College, Toronto, with the Degree of Bachelor of Arts, and was chosen Professor of Mathematics in St. Mary's Ladies' College, at Dallas, Texas.   She subsequently resigned in order to attend upon her sister who was seriously ill.

25   **Jessie Margarita Potts,**[4] (George Jerald,[3] Alexander,[2] John,[1]), daughter of Dr. George Jerald and Agnes (Stewart) Potts, is a clever musican, and resides at home with her parents.

INDEX
To Names of Persons.

INDEX.

Part I. The Potts Family in Great Britain.

(659)

84

INDEX.

Part II. The Potts Family in America.

NOTE. Surnames, other than Potts, only are given. The tabulated pedigrees are only partially indexed. Where the same name occurs on consecutive pages, the first and last pages, joined by a hyphen, is sometimes given.

85

86

INDEX.

Part III.   David Potts and his Descendants.

NOTE. For the sake classification, as well as convenience, this Index is divided into three groups:—First, names of descendants of David Potts ; Second, names of those who have married descendants ; Third, surnames of persons casually named.

88

WALKER,

1209 Emma, 556.
1183 Enos, 555.
1212 George, 557.
275 Hannah, 484.
1702 Havard, 588.
278 Isaac, 484.
565 Isaac, 509, 555.
1186 Isaac S., 555.
279 Jane, 484.
1207 Jane, 556.
990 Jesse Wager, 535, 588.
271 Joseph Burden, 484.
276 Joseph Burden, 484.
571 Joshua Vale, 509, 556.
1180 Julia Ann, 555.
1182 Lewis, 555.
568 Louisa, 509, 556.
1208 Lydia, 556.
281 Mary, 484.
1213 Mary, 557.
569 Mary Ann, 509.
991 Mary Jane, 535.
1704 Miriam Kempster, 589.
1184 Morris, 555.
570 Morris E., 509, 556.
1179 Peter D., 555.
567 Priscilla, 509, 556.
1185 Rebecca Jane, 555.
273 Richard Currie, 484.
1703 Roland, 588.
272 Sarah, 484.
572 Sarah, 509, 557.
1705 Walter Havard, 589.
1211 Warren B., 556.
274 William, 484.
993 William Potts, 535, 588.
280 Zillah, 484.

WALTON,

466 Elizabeth, 497.
463 John, 497.

WALTON,

462 Mary, 497.
461 Pierce, 497.
465 Sarah, 497.
464 William, 497.

WATKINS,

1902 Fred A., 613.

WATTERSON,

1740 Alice C., 492.
1739 Florence, 492.
1738 M. Louetta, 492.
1737 R. Belle, 492.
1741 Walter D., 492.

WEBSTER

1623 Clarkson Lukens, 582.
1624 Edith, 582.
1622 Edward Burroughs, 582.
1626 J. Howard, 582.
1625 J. Percival, 582.

WEIK,

1490 Anna M., 573.
1491 John, 573.
1489 Louisa, 573, 609.

WELLS,

1399 Clara, 567.
1400 Harriet, 567.
1395 Ida, 567.
1394 Mary E., 567.
1396 Minerva, 567.
1397 Morris T., 567.
1398 Viola, 567.

WENTWORTH,

1452 Adele, 570.
1451 Stanley, 570.

WENTZ,

1872 Thomas, 609.

WHITE,

819 Anna M., 525.

91

Part III, Continued. Names of Persons Who Have Married Descendants of David Potts.

Abbott, Henry, 620-e.
Acuff, Anne, 481.
Adams, Albyn L., 620-h.
Adamson, Rebecca J., 526, 577.
Aiken, Jennie, 532, 584.
Allen, Mary, 546, 595.
Altemus, Daniel, 484, 515.
Ambruster, Jacob M., 499.
Ammon, Zilpha, 526, 577.
Ansby, Sarah, 486, 519.
Armstrong, John, 582, 611.
Armstrong, William A., 582.
Ashmead, Ann, 454, 463.
Austin, Theresa, 527, 579.

Badger, Henrietta M., 489, 520.
Bailey, Francis, 530, 583.
Baker, Joseph B., 536, 589.
Baker, Lydell, 620-g.
Baker, Rachel, 462, 475.
Baker, William, 502, 545.
Baldwin, Mercy, 471, 491.
Baldwin, Theodore A., 543, 592.
Balfour, George, 620-b, 620-c.
Barnes, George, 528, 578.
Barnes, William, 527.
Barnhill, Robert, 462, 474.
Barton, William, 518.
Bates, Annie M., 587.
Bates, Mary, 580.
Baynes, Fannie, 535, 588.
Beach, Louis, 571.
Beans, Joseph, 486.

Beard, Susan, 519, 569.
Beatty, Sadie Grace, 548, 599.
Belch, John, 482, 513.
Bell, William, 573, 609.
Benezole, Ann, 520.
Benham, Vincent, 478, 505.
Bennett, Edith T., 535.
Bentley, Sheshbazzar, 480, 510.
Bickins, Charles, 523.
Biedler, Elizabeth, 484.
Bilger, Emma, 489, 522.
Black, David, 519, 568.
Blackburn, J. K., 510.
Blackburn, Jonah, 482.
Blackford, John, 510.
Blair, George, 620-d.
Blair, Marion E., 549, 601.
Blane, Lyda, 565, 605.
Blymyer, Eliza, 485, 518.
Boone, Arnold, 476.
Boring, Sarah, 569, 606.
Bosenbury, Philip, 508, 554.
Boyer, Anna, 542, 590.
Boyer, Mary, 543, 591.
Bracken, Clara, 511.
Bracken, Rebecca, 511, 558.
Brant, Ann, 485, 517.
Brevoort, Alice, 500, 541.
Brevoort, ——, 500, 542.
Broadess, William, 470.
Brognard, L. N., 524, 573.
Brook, Amanda, 527, 578.

Part III, Continued. Surnames of Persons Incidentally Mentioned.

P. 474, No 170

[illegible] Barnhill [illegible]

[illegible]

Father of Theodore Roosevelt

father of THEODORE ROOSEVEL[illegible]

CPSIA information can be obtained
at www.ICGtesting.com
Printed in the USA
LVHW030731221218
600915LV00007B/382/P